interchange

FIFTH EDITION

Student's Book

intro B

Jack C. Richards

WITH DIGITAL PACK

CAMBRIDGE UNIVERSITY PRESS

CAMBRIDGE
UNIVERSITY PRESS & ASSESSMENT

Shaftesbury Road, Cambridge CB2 8EA, United Kingdom

One Liberty Plaza, 20th Floor, New York, NY 10006, USA

477 Williamstown Road, Port Melbourne, VIC 3207, Australia

314–321, 3rd Floor, Plot 3, Splendor Forum, Jasola District Centre, New Delhi – 110025, India

103 Penang Road, #05-06/07, Visioncrest Commercial, Singapore 238467

Cambridge University Press & Assessment is a department of the University of Cambridge.

We share the University's mission to contribute to society through the pursuit of education, learning and research at the highest international levels of excellence.

www.cambridge.org
Information on this title: www.cambridge.org/9781009040570

First published 2013
Fifth edition 2017
Fifth edition update published 2022

20 19 18 17 16 15 14 13 12 11 10 9 8 7 6 5 4 3 2

Printed in Poland by Opolgraf

A catalogue record for this publication is available from the British Library

ISBN 978-1-009-04041-9 Intro Student's Book with eBook
ISBN 978-1-009-04042-6 Intro Student's Book A with eBook
ISBN 978-1-009-04043-3 Intro Student's Book B with eBook
ISBN 978-1-009-04055-6 Intro Student's Book with Digital Pack
ISBN 978-1-009-04056-3 Intro Student's Book A with Digital Pack
ISBN 978-1-009-04057-0 Intro Student's Book B with Digital Pack
ISBN 978-1-316-62237-7 Intro Workbook
ISBN 978-1-316-62239-1 Intro Workbook A
ISBN 978-1-316-62240-7 Intro Workbook B
ISBN 978-1-108-40605-5 Intro Teacher's Edition
ISBN 978-1-316-62221-6 Intro Class Audio
ISBN 978-1-009-04058-7 Intro Full Contact with Digital Pack
ISBN 978-1-009-04059-4 Intro Full Contact A with Digital Pack
ISBN 978-1-009-04062-4 Intro Full Contact B with Digital Pack
ISBN 978-1-108-40304-7 Presentation Plus Intro

Additional resources for this publication at cambridgeone.org

Informed by teachers

Teachers from all over the world helped develop *Interchange Fifth Edition*. They looked at everything – from the color of the designs to the topics in the conversations – in order to make sure that this course will work in the classroom. We heard from 1,500 teachers in:

- Surveys
- Focus Groups
- In-Depth Reviews

We appreciate the help and input from everyone. In particular, we'd like to give the following people our special thanks:

Jader Franceschi, **Actúa Idiomas,** Bento Gonçalves, Rio Grande do Sul, Brazil

Juliana Dos Santos Voltan Costa, **Actus Idiomas,** São Paulo, Brazil

Ella Osorio, **Angelo State University,** San Angelo, TX, US

Mary Hunter, **Angelo State University,** San Angelo, TX, US

Mario César González, **Angloamericano de Monterrey, SC,** Monterrey, Mexico

Samantha Shipman, **Auburn High School,** Auburn, AL, US

Linda, **Bernick Language School,** Radford, VA, US

Dave Lowrance, **Bethesda University of California,** Yorba Linda, CA, US

Tajbakhsh Hosseini, **Bezmialem Vakif University,** Istanbul, Turkey

Dilek Gercek, **Bil English,** Izmir, Turkey

erkan kolat, **Biruni University, ELT,** Istanbul, Turkey

Nika Gutkowska, **Bluedata International,** New York, NY, US

Daniel Alcocer Gómez, **Cecati 92,** Guadalupe, Nuevo León, Mexico

Samantha Webb, **Central Middle School,** Milton-Freewater, OR, US

Verónica Salgado, **Centro Anglo Americano,** Cuernavaca, Mexico

Ana Rivadeneira Martínez and Georgia P. de Machuca, **Centro de Educación Continua – Universidad Politécnica del Ecuador,** Quito, Ecuador

Anderson Francisco Guimerães Maia, **Centro Cultural Brasil Estados Unidos,** Belém, Brazil

Rosana Mariano, **Centro Paula Souza,** São Paulo, Brazil

Carlos de la Paz Arroyo, Teresa Noemí Parra Alarcón, Gilberto

Bastida Gaytan, Manuel Esquivel Román, and Rosa Cepeda Tapia, **Centro Universitario Angloamericano,** Cuernavaca, Morelos, Mexico

Antonio Almeida, **CETEC,** Morelos, Mexico

Cinthia Ferreira, **Cinthia Ferreira Languages Services,** Toronto, ON, Canada

Phil Thomas and Sérgio Sanchez, **CLS Canadian Language School,** São Paulo, Brazil

Celia Concannon, **Cochise College,** Nogales, AZ, US

Maria do Carmo Rocha and CAOP English team, **Colégio Arquidiocesano Ouro Preto – Unidade Cônego Paulo Dilascio,** Ouro Preto, Brazil

Kim Rodriguez, **College of Charleston North,** Charleston, SC, US

Jesús Leza Alvarado, **Coparmex English Institute,** Monterrey, Mexico

John Partain, **Cortazar,** Guanajuato, Mexico

Alexander Palencia Navas, **Cursos de Lenguas, Universidad del Atlántico,** Barranquilla, Colombia

Kenneth Johan Gerardo Steenhuisen Cera, Melfi Osvaldo Guzman Triana, and Carlos Alberto Algarín Jiminez, **Cursos de Lenguas Extranjeras Universidad del Atlantico,** Barranquilla, Colombia

Jane P Kerford, **East Los Angeles College,** Pasadena, CA, US

Daniela, **East Village,** Campinas, São Paulo

Rosalva Camacho Orduño, **Easy English for Groups S.A. de C.V.,** Monterrey, Nuevo León, Mexico

Adonis Gimenez Fusetti, **Easy Way Idiomas,** Ibiúna, Brazil

Eileen Thompson, **Edison Community College,** Piqua, OH, US

Ahminne Handeri O.L Froede, **Englishouse escola de idiomas,** Teófilo Otoni, Brazil

Ana Luz Delgado-Izazola, **Escuela Nacional Preparatoria 5, UNAM,** Mexico City, Mexico

Nancy Alarcón Mendoza, **Facultad de Estudios Superiores Zaragoza, UNAM,** Mexico City, Mexico

Marcilio N. Barros, **Fast English USA,** Campinas, São Paulo, Brazil

Greta Douthat, **FCI Ashland,** Ashland, KY, US

Carlos Lizárraga González, **Grupo Educativo Anglo Americano, S.C.,** Mexico City, Mexico

Hugo Fernando Alcántar Valle, **Instituto Politécnico Nacional, Escuela Superior de Comercio y Administración-Unidad Santotomás, Celex Esca Santo Tomás,** Mexico City, Mexico

Sueli Nascimento, **Instituto Superior de Educação do Rio de Janeiro,** Rio de Janeiro, Brazil

Elsa F Monteverde, **International Academic Services,** Miami, FL, US

Laura Anand, **Irvine Adult School,** Irvine, CA, US

Prof. Marli T. Fernandes (principal) and Prof. Dr. Jefferson J. Fernandes (pedagogue), **Jefferson Idiomass,** São Paulo, Brazil

Herman Bartelen, **Kanda Gaigo Gakuin,** Tokyo, Japan

Cassia Silva, **Key Languages,** Key Biscayne, FL, US

Sister Mary Hope, **Kyoto Notre Dame Joshi Gakuin,** Kyoto, Japan

Nate Freedman, **LAL Language Centres,** Boston, MA, US

Richard Janzen, **Langley Secondary School,** Abbotsford, BC, Canada

Christina Abel Gabardo, **Language House,** Campo Largo, Brazil
Ivonne Castro, **Learn English International,** Cali, Colombia
Julio Cesar Maciel Rodrigues, **Liberty Centro de Línguas,** São Paulo, Brazil
Ann Gibson, **Maynard High School,** Maynard, MA, US
Martin Darling, **Meiji Gakuin Daigaku,** Tokyo, Japan
Dax Thomas, **Meiji Gakuin Daigaku,** Yokohama, Kanagawa, Japan
Derya Budak, **Mevlana University,** Konya, Turkey
B Sullivan, **Miami Valley Career Technical Center International Program,** Dayton, OH, US
Julio Velazquez, **Milo Language Center,** Weston, FL, US
Daiane Siqueira da Silva, Luiz Carlos Buontempo, Marlete Avelina de Oliveira Cunha, Marcos Paulo Segatti, Morgana Eveline de Oliveira, Nadia Lia Gino Alo, and Paul Hyde Budgen, **New Interchange-Escola de Idiomas,** São Paulo, Brazil
Patrícia França Furtado da Costa, Juiz de Fora, Brazil
Patricia Servín
Chris Pollard, **North West Regional College SK,** North Battleford, SK, Canada
Olga Amy, **Notre Dame High School,** Red Deer, Canada
Amy Garrett, **Ouachita Baptist University,** Arkadelphia, AR, US
Mervin Curry, **Palm Beach State College,** Boca Raton, FL, US
Julie Barros, **Quality English Studio,** Guarulhos, São Paulo, Brazil
Teodoro González Saldaña and Jesús Monserrrta Mata Franco, **Race Idiomas,** Mexico City, Mexico
Autumn Westphal and Noga La`or, **Rennert International,** New York, NY, US
Antonio Gallo and Javy Palau, **Rigby Idiomas,** Monterrey, Mexico Tatiane Gabriela Sperb do Nascimento, **Right Way,** Igrejinha, Brazil
Mustafa Akgül, **Selahaddin Eyyubi Universitesi,** Diyarbakır, Turkey
James Drury M. Fonseca, **Senac Idiomas Fortaleza,** Fortaleza, Ceara, Brazil
Manoel Fialho S Neto, **Senac – PE,** Recife, Brazil
Jane Imber, **Small World,** Lawrence, KS, US
Tony Torres, **South Texas College,** McAllen, TX, US
Janet Rose, **Tennessee Foreign Language Institute,** College Grove, TN, US
Todd Enslen, **Tohoku University,** Sendai, Miyagi, Japan
Daniel Murray, **Torrance Adult School,** Torrance, CA, US
Juan Manuel Pulido Mendoza, **Universidad del Atlántico,** Barranquilla, Colombia
Juan Carlos Vargas Millán, **Universidad Libre Seccional Cali,** Cali (Valle del Cauca), Colombia
Carmen Cecilia Llanos Ospina, **Universidad Libre Seccional Cali,** Cali, Colombia
Jorge Noriega Zenteno, **Universidad Politécnica del Valle de México,** Estado de México, Mexico
Aimee Natasha Holguin S., **Universidad Politécnica del Valle de México UPVM,** Tultitlàn Estado de México, Mexico
Christian Selene Bernal Barraza, **UPVM Universidad Politécnica del Valle de México,** Ecatepec, Mexico
Lizeth Ramos Acosta, **Universidad Santiago de Cali,** Cali, Colombia
Silvana Dushku, **University of Illinois Champaign,** IL, US
Deirdre McMurtry, **University of Nebraska – Omaha,** Omaha, NE, US
Jason E Mower, **University of Utah,** Salt Lake City, UT, US
Paul Chugg, **Vanguard Taylor Language Institute,** Edmonton, Alberta, Canada
Henry Mulak, **Varsity Tutors,** Los Angeles, CA, US
Shirlei Strucker Calgaro and Hugo Guilherme Karrer, **VIP Centro de Idiomas,** Panambi, Rio Grande do Sul, Brazil
Eleanor Kelly, **Waseda Daigaku Extension Centre,** Tokyo, Japan
Sherry Ashworth, **Wichita State University,** Wichita, KS, US
Laine Bourdene, **William Carey University,** Hattiesburg, MS, US
Serap Aydın, Istanbul, Turkey
Liliana Covino, Guarulhos, Brazil
Yannuarys Jiménez, Barranquilla, Colombia
Juliana Morais Pazzini, Toronto, ON, Canada
Marlon Sanches, Montreal, Canada

Additional content contributed by Kenna Bourke, Inara Couto, Nic Harris, Greg Manin, Ashleigh Martinez, Laura McKenzie, Paul McIntyre, Clara Prado, Lynne Robertson, Mari Vargo, Theo Walker, and Maria Lucia Zaorob.

Classroom Language Teacher instructions

Plan of Intro Book B

Pronunciation/Listening	Writing/Reading	Interchange Activity
Sentence stress Listening for people's food preferences	Writing about mealtime habits "It's a Food Festival!": Reading about foods people celebrate	"Planning a party": Choose snacks for a party and compare answers **PAGE 123**
Pronunciation of *can* and *can't* Listening for people's favorite sports to watch or play; listening to people talk about their abilities	Writing questions about sports "Awesome Sports Records": Reading about fitness records from around the world	"Hidden talents": Finding out more about your classmates' hidden talents **PAGE 124**
Reduction of *going to* Listening to people talk about their holiday plans	Writing about weekend plans "Happy Birthday to You!": Reading about birthday customs in different places	"Take a guess": Making guesses about a classmate's plans **PAGE 125**
Sentence intonation Listening to people talk about health problems; listening for medications	Writing advice for health problems "Do You Know Your Body?": Reading interesting facts about your body	"Problems, problems": Giving advice for some common problems **PAGE 126**
Compound nouns Listening to people talk about shopping; listening to directions	Writing directions "A Tour of Palermo, Buenos Aires": Reading about popular tourist attractions in Buenos Aires, Argentina	"Giving directions": Asking for directions in a neighborhood **PAGE 127, 128**
Simple past *-ed* endings Listening to people talk about their past summer activities	Writing about last weekend "Did You Have a Good Weekend?": Reading about four people's weekend experiences	"Past activities": Comparing your classmates' childhoods **PAGE 129**
Negative contractions Listening for places and dates of birth	Writing questions about a person's life "Who is Marina Chapman?": Reading about a woman's life	"This is your life": Finding out more about your classmates' lives **PAGE 130**
Reduction of *want to* and *have to* Listening to phone conversations about making and changing plans	Writing about weekend plans "Austin City Limits!": Reading about events at a festival	"The perfect weekend": Making plans with your classmates **PAGE 131**

9 I always eat breakfast.

- Discuss food
- Describe eating habits

1 WORD POWER Foods

A Listen and practice.

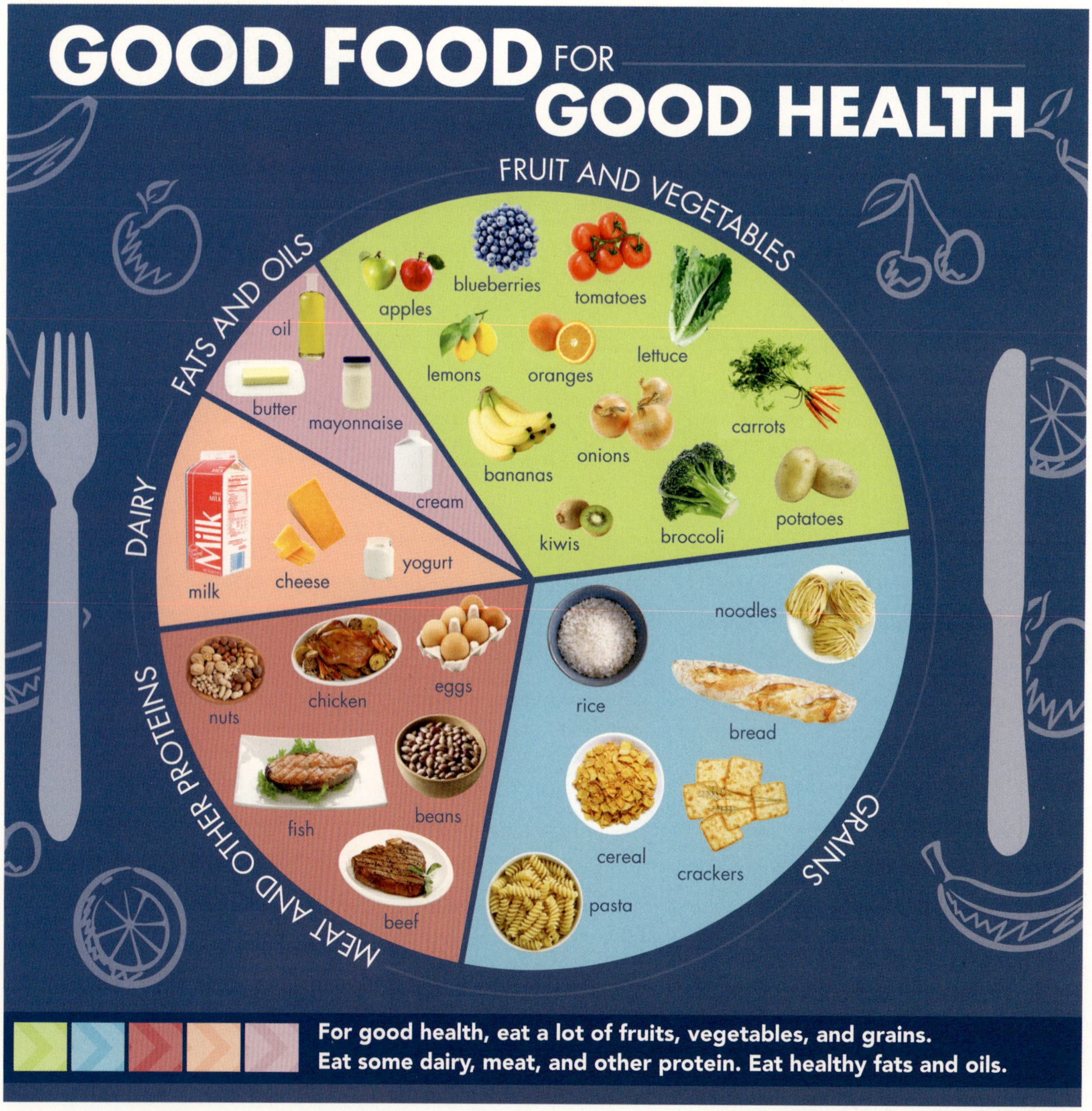

B **PAIR WORK** What foods do you like? What don't you like? Make a list. Then tell a partner.

A: I like chicken, potatoes, and apples. I don't like beef, broccoli, or onions.

B: I like . . .

I like	I don't like
chicken	beef
potatoes	broccoli
apples	onions

2 CONVERSATION Let's get some lettuce and some tomatoes.

Listen and practice.

Keith Do we need any lettuce for the sandwiches?

Jane Good idea. Let's get some lettuce and some tomatoes.

Keith Do we have any bread?

Jane No, we need some. And we don't have any cheese.

Keith Let's get some cheese, then. And some chicken, too.

Jane We have some chicken at home.

Keith Oh, all right. How about some potato salad?

Jane Sure. I love potato salad.

Keith Great! Let's buy some.

3 GRAMMAR FOCUS

Count and noncount nouns; *some* and *any*

Count nouns	Noncount nouns
an egg → egg**s**	bread
a potato → potato**es**	lettuce
Do we need **any** potatoes?	Do we need **any** lettuce?
Yes. Let's get **some** (potatoes).	Yes. Let's get **some** (lettuce).
No. We don't need **any** (potatoes).	No. We don't need **any** (lettuce).

GRAMMAR PLUS see page 140

A Complete the conversation with *some* or *any*.

Keith Oh, they don't have ___any___ potato salad.
Jane But we have lots of potatoes at home. Let's make ___________.
Keith Great. Do we have ___________ mayonnaise?
Jane No. We need to buy ___________. And we need ___________ onions.
Keith Oh, no, I don't want ___________ onions in the salad.
Jane OK, don't worry. Let's get ___________ celery, then.
Keith No, I don't want ___________ celery. I have an idea. Let's put ___________ apples in it.
Jane Are you serious? Apples in potato salad? Well, OK . . .

B Complete the chart with foods from Exercise 1. Then compare with a partner.

Count			Noncount		
crackers			bread		

4 PRONUNCIATION Sentence stress

A Listen and practice. Notice the stressed words.

A: Do we need any beans?
B: Yes. We need some beans.

A: Do we need any rice?
B: No. We don't need any rice.

B **PAIR WORK** Ask *Do we need . . . ?* questions about the food in the picture. Then look at the shopping list and answer.

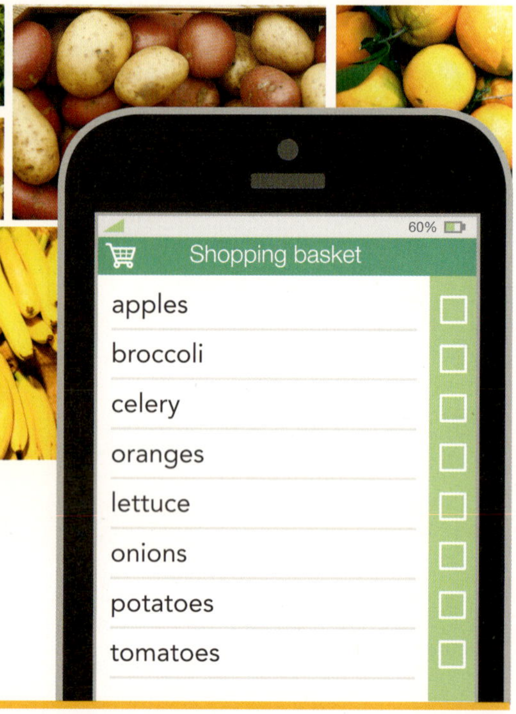

A: Do we need any apples?
B: Yes. We need some apples. Do we need any bananas?
A: Let's see . . . No, we don't need any bananas.

5 SNAPSHOT

Listen and practice.

BREAKFAST AROUND THE WORLD

THE UNITED STATES	JAPAN	COSTA RICA
☐ cereal with milk	☐ fish	☐ rice and beans
☐ fresh fruit	☐ rice	☐ eggs
☐ orange juice	☐ soup	☐ red peppers
☐ coffee	☐ pickles	☐ bananas
☐ pastries	☐ green tea	☐ coffee with milk

What do you have for breakfast? Check (✓) the foods and drinks.
What else do you have for breakfast?

6 CONVERSATION We always have green tea.

Listen and practice.

Eva: What is a typical Japanese breakfast, Kaito?

Kaito: Well, we usually have fish, rice, and soup.

Eva: Fish for breakfast? That's interesting.

Kaito: Oh, it's really good. Sometimes we have a salad, too. But we never have coffee.

Eva: Really? What do you have?

Kaito: We always have green tea.

Eva: I love green tea!

Kaito: Listen, my family usually has a Japanese-style breakfast on weekends. Why don't you come to my house on Sunday?

Eva: That's very nice of you. Thanks!

7 GRAMMAR FOCUS

Adverbs of frequency

I **always** / **usually** / **often** / **sometimes** / **hardly ever** / **never** eat breakfast.	Do you **ever** have fish for breakfast?	100% **always**
	Yes, I **always** do.	**usually**
	Sometimes I do.	**often**
	No, I **never** do.	**sometimes**
		hardly ever
Sometimes I eat breakfast.		0% **never**

GRAMMAR PLUS see page 140

A Put the adverbs in the correct places. Then practice with a partner.

A: Do you ^usually^ have a big breakfast? (usually)
B: Well, on Sunday I have a big breakfast with my friends. (always)
A: Do you eat breakfast at work on weekdays? (ever)
B: Yes, I have breakfast at the office restaurant. (sometimes)
A: Do you eat breakfast at your desk? (often)
B: No, I eat breakfast at my desk. (hardly ever)

B Unscramble the sentences.

1. I / have / hardly ever / beef / for lunch   *I hardly ever have beef for lunch.*
2. when I watch TV / I / snacks / eat / never   ____________
3. eat / for / eggs / breakfast / sometimes / I   ____________
4. have / I / dinner / with / usually / family / my   ____________

C Rewrite the sentences from part B with your own information. Then compare with a partner.

A: I usually have beef or chicken for lunch.
B: I never have beef. I don't like it. I often have fish and a salad for lunch.

8 LISTENING Carrots are my favorite!

A Devon and Victoria are talking about food. How often does Victoria eat these foods? Listen and check (✓) Often, Sometimes, or Never.

	OFTEN	SOMETIMES	NEVER
noodles	✓		
chicken			
fish			
eggs			
carrots			

B **GROUP WORK** Do you ever eat the foods in part A? Tell your classmates.

A: I often eat noodles.
B: Really? I never eat noodles.
C: Well, I . . .

9 SPEAKING Mealtime survey

A Add two questions about mealtime habits to the chart. Then ask two people the questions. Write their names and complete the chart.

	Name:	Name:
1. Do you always have a big breakfast?		
2. What time do you usually have lunch?		
3. What do you usually have for lunch?		
4. Do you often have snacks in the afternoon?		
5. Do you ever go to a restaurant for dinner?		
6. What's something you never eat for dinner?		
7. ______________________________?		
8. ______________________________?		

A: Pedro, do you always have a big breakfast?
B: No, I hardly ever do. I have coffee and milk. Sometimes I eat bread or crackers.

B **CLASS ACTIVITY** Tell your classmates about your partners' mealtime habits.

"Pedro hardly ever has a big breakfast. But he always eats lunch and dinner . . . "

10 INTERCHANGE 9 Planning a party

Decide what food and drinks to serve at a party. Go to Interchange 9 on page 123.

11 READING

A Look at the pictures. Which foods do you like?

IT'S A FOOD Festival!

LA TOMATINA

People usually eat tomatoes. But once a year, in Buñol, Spain, people just throw them! Yes, that's correct. The whole town of Buñol has a giant tomato fight! It's very messy. By the end of the day, there are squashed tomatoes all over town. In fact, there are 120 tons of squashed tomatoes!

GARLIC FESTIVAL

All over the world, people use garlic in their cooking. Some people in California, in the U.S., really like garlic. They like it so much that every year they celebrate it with a garlic festival. You can taste garlic in everything you can think of. There's even garlic ice cream and garlic popcorn.

MONKEY BUFFET FESTIVAL

There's something very interesting about this food festival. It's not for people, it's for monkeys! In Lopburi, Thailand, people bring all kinds of different fruits and leave them out for the monkeys to eat. They bring pineapples, apples, mangoes . . . and bananas, of course. It's the people's way of saying thank you to the monkeys. That's because tourists come to see the monkeys, and that helps the people's businesses. Isn't that cool?

BREAD FOR THE DAY OF THE DEAD

The Day of the Dead is a very important day in Mexico. Many people celebrate their family members and friends by baking special bread. They make bread in the shape of humans, flowers, bones, and animals. The bread is sweet, and sometimes it has anise seeds or orange in it.

B Read the article. Then correct these sentences.

1. There's a big tomato fight in ~~Mexico~~ Spain once a year.
2. People in California don't like garlic.
3. Some people in the U.S. use tomatoes to make ice cream and popcorn.
4. The Monkey Buffet Festival happens in Spain.
5. In Thailand, people give fruit to the tourists.
6. Some Mexicans make bread in the shape of houses and other buildings.

C **GROUP WORK** Do you eat any special food at celebrations in your country? What do you celebrate and which foods do you eat? Tell your classmates.

10 What sports do you like?

- Discuss sports to watch and play
- Discuss skills, abilities, and talents

1 SNAPSHOT

Listen and practice.

SPORTS QUIZ

Brazil's favorite sport is soccer. Their second favorite is . . .

- ☐ tennis
- ☐ volleyball
- ☐ swimming

Mexico's favorite sport is soccer. Their second favorite sport is . . .

- ☐ football
- ☐ hockey
- ☐ baseball

Canada's favorite sport is ice hockey. Their second favorite sport is . . .

- ☐ basketball
- ☐ ice-skating
- ☐ snowboarding

South Korea's favorite sport is basketball. Their second favorite sport is . . .

- ☐ bike riding
- ☐ hiking
- ☐ soccer

Brazil: volleyball; Mexico: baseball; Canada: basketball; South Korea: soccer

Can you guess what sports are the second favorite in each country? Check (✓) the sports.
Do you like sports? What sports are popular in your country?

2 CONVERSATION When do you play all these sports?

Listen and practice.

TARA So, Victor, what do you do in your free time?

VICTOR Well, I really like sports.

TARA Cool! What sports do you like?

VICTOR My favorite sports are basketball, soccer, and tennis.

TARA Wow! You're a really good athlete. When do you play all these sports?

VICTOR Oh . . . I don't play them very often.

TARA What do you mean?

VICTOR I just watch them on TV!

3 GRAMMAR FOCUS

Simple present Wh-questions

What sports do you play?	I play **soccer and basketball**.
Who do you play basketball **with**?	I play **with some friends from work**.
Where do you play?	We play **at a gym near the office**.
How often do you practice?	We practice **twice a week**.
When do you practice?	We practice **on Tuesdays and Thursdays**.
What time do you start?	We start **at six in the evening**.

GRAMMAR PLUS *see page 141*

A Complete the conversations with the correct Wh-question words. Then practice with a partner.

1. **A:** ___How often___ do you go bike riding?
   B: Oh, about once or twice a week.
   A: I love to go bike riding. I go every Sunday.
   B: Really? ______________ do you go?
   A: Usually at about ten in the morning.
   B: Oh, yeah? ______________ do you go with?
   A: A group of friends. Come with us next time!
2. **A:** I watch sports on TV every weekend.
   B: Really? ______________ do you like to watch?
   A: Soccer. It's my favorite!
   B: ______________ do you usually watch soccer?
   A: In the evening or on weekends.
   B: And ______________ do you usually watch it? At home?
   A: No, at my brother's house. He has a home theater!

B Complete the conversation with Wh-questions. Then compare with a partner.

A: ___What sports do you like___?
B: I like a lot of sports, but I really love volleyball!
A: ______________________________?
B: I usually play with my sister and some friends.
A: ______________________________?
B: We practice on Saturdays.
A: ______________________________?
B: We start at about noon.
A: ______________________________?
B: We usually play at a sports club, but sometimes we play on the beach.

C **PAIR WORK** Ask your partner five questions about sports or other activities. Then tell the class.

A: What sports do you like?
B: I don't like sports very much.
A: Oh? What do you like to do in your free time?

4 LISTENING What do you think of sports?

Listen to the conversations about sports. Complete the chart.

	Favorite sport	Do they play or watch it? Play	Watch
1. James	football	☑	☐
2. Brianna		☐	☐
3. Matthew		☐	☐
4. Nicole		☐	☐

5 SPEAKING Free-time activities

A Add one more question about free-time activities to the chart. Then ask two people the questions. Write their names and complete the chart.

	Name:	Name:
1. What sports do you like to watch or play?		
2. What do you do on the weekends?		
3. What do you like to do when the weather is nice?		
4. What do you like to do when it's raining?		
5. How often do you play video games?		
6. ______________________________?		

A: Soo-hyun, what sports do you like?
B: I like a lot of sports. My favorites are soccer and baseball.

B **CLASS ACTIVITY** Tell your classmates about your partners' free-time activities.

6 CONVERSATION What can I do?

Listen and practice.

Dylan Look! There's a talent show audition on Friday. Let's enter.
Becky Oh, I can't enter a talent show. What can I do?
Dylan You can sing very well.
Becky Really? Thanks!
Dylan I can't sing at all, but I can play the piano, so . . .
Becky So maybe we can enter the contest.
Dylan Of course we can. Let's do it!
Becky OK. We can practice tomorrow!

7 GRAMMAR FOCUS

Can for ability

I				you			I		What **can** I do?
You				I			you		You **can** sing.
She	**can**	sing very well.	**Can**	she	sing?	Yes,	she	**can**.	
He	**can't**	sing at all.		he		No,	he	**can't**.	Who **can** sing?
We				we			we		Becky **can**.
They				they			they		

GRAMMAR PLUS see page 141

A Six people are talking about things they can and can't do. Complete these sentences.

Ben

1. I ___*can*___ swim.

Sara

2. I ____________ fix cars.

Diane

3. I ____________ sing.

Jeff

4. I ____________ ice-skate.

Lisa

5. I ____________ play the piano.

Megan

6. I ____________ cook.

B PAIR WORK Ask and answer questions about the pictures in part A.

A: Can Ben swim?
B: Yes, he can.

C GROUP WORK Can your classmates do the things in part A? Ask and answer questions.

"Can you swim, Diego?"

8 PRONUNCIATION *Can* and *can't*

A Listen and practice. Notice the pronunciation of **can** and **can't**.

/kən/	/kænt/
I **can** play the piano.	I **can't** sing at all.

B PAIR WORK Your partner reads a sentence for each number. Check (✓) the sentence you hear.

1. ☐ I can cook.
   ☐ I can't cook.
2. ☐ I can drive.
   ☐ I can't drive.
3. ☐ I can swim.
   ☐ I can't swim.
4. ☐ I can dance.
   ☐ I can't dance.

9 LISTENING Are you good at sports?

Listen to three people talk about their abilities. Write J (Joshua), M (Monica), or A (Anthony) on the things they can do well.

10 WORD POWER Talents and abilities

A Complete the word map with talents and abilities from the list. Then listen and practice.

- ✓ bake cookies
- build a robot
- design a website
- do math in your head
- edit a video
- fix a computer
- make electronic music
- play chess
- ride a horse
- run a marathon
- skateboard
- take good photos
- tell good jokes

B **GROUP WORK** Who can do the things in part A? Make a list of guesses about your classmates.

A: Who can bake cookies?
B: I think Melanie can.
C: Who can design . . . ?

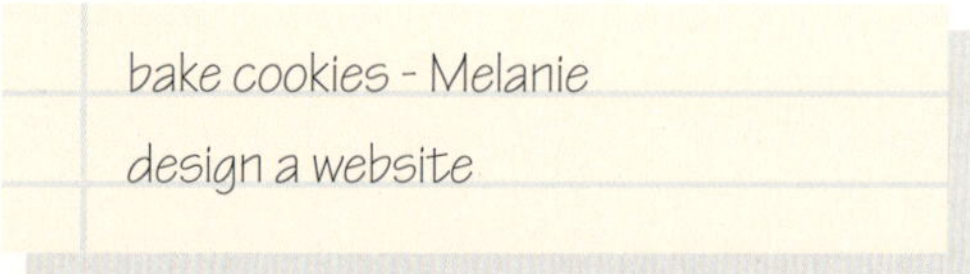

C **CLASS ACTIVITY** Go around the room and check your guesses.

A: Melanie, can you bake cookies?
B: Yes, I can.

11 INTERCHANGE 10 Hidden talents and abilities

Learn more about your classmates' hidden talents and abilities. Go to Interchange 10 on page 124.

12 READING

A Some people like to set world records. Why do you think they like to do that?

Awesome Sports Records

base jumping

Base jumping is a dangerous sport. People jump off buildings, bridges, and other high places. The Burj Khalifa tower in Dubai, United Arab Emirates, is 824 meters (2,717 feet) tall. That's a very scary jump. But Fred Fugen and Vince Reffet of France can jump it! They also enjoy skydiving and parachuting.

Do you know what a unicycle is? It's a bicycle with just one wheel. David Weichenberger of Austria has the world record for longest jump on a unicycle. He can jump 2.95 meters (about 10 feet).

Kalamandalam Hemalatha of India has an amazing marathon record, but it's not for running. She can dance, and dance, and dance! In fact, Kalamandalam can dance for 123 hours and 15 minutes. That's the longest dance marathon on record. Kalamandalam's special dance is from India. It's called the Mohiniyattam dance.

Mohiniyattam dance

Otto the skateboarding dog

Do you know about Otto? Otto likes surfing, skateboarding, and playing soccer. Otto is a champion skateboarder, but he's a dog from Lima, Peru! Otto has the record for skateboarding through the legs of 30 people!

Can you squash an apple? Can you squash it using just the muscles in your arms? One woman can! Her name is Linsey Lindberg. Linsey is from Texas, in the U.S. In one minute, she can squash 10 apples. That's one apple every six seconds.

B Read the records. Then check (✓) the correct answers to the questions.

1. What's special about a unicycle?
   - ☐ **a.** It has no wheels. ☐ **b.** It has one wheel, not two.
2. Who likes base jumping?
   - ☐ **a.** David Weichenberger ☐ **b.** Fred Fugen
3. What sort of marathon can Kalamandalam do?
   - ☐ **a.** a dance marathon ☐ **b.** a running marathon
4. How does Linsey Lindberg squash apples?
   - ☐ **a.** with her hands ☐ **b.** with her arm muscles
5. What is one sport that Otto plays?
   - ☐ **a.** basketball ☐ **b.** soccer

C **GROUP WORK** Do you think it's fun to set world records? Why or why not? What other world records do you know about? Tell your classmates.

Units 9–10 Progress check

SELF-ASSESSMENT

How well can you do these things? Check (✓) the boxes.

I can . . .	Very well	OK	A little
Make and respond to suggestions (Ex. 1)	☐	☐	☐
Talk about food and drink (Ex. 1, 2)	☐	☐	☐
Ask and answer questions about eating habits (Ex. 2)	☐	☐	☐
Understand descriptions of sporting activities (Ex. 3)	☐	☐	☐
Ask and answer questions about likes and dislikes (Ex. 4)	☐	☐	☐
Talk about job abilities (Ex. 5)	☐	☐	☐

1 SPEAKING Planning a class party

A **GROUP WORK** Plan a class party. Choose two main dishes, two salads, two drinks, and two desserts. Then tell the class.

Main dishes		
Salads		
Drinks		
Desserts		

useful expressions

Do we want any . . . ?
Let's get/make some . . .
I don't want/like . . .
Everybody likes . . .

2 SPEAKING Movie snacks

PAIR WORK Does your partner ever have these snacks at the movies? Add one more snack to the chart. Ask questions and complete the survey.

	Always	Usually	Sometimes	Hardly ever	Never
1. candy	☐	☐	☐	☐	☐
2. coffee	☐	☐	☐	☐	☐
3. pizza	☐	☐	☐	☐	☐
4. popcorn	☐	☐	☐	☐	☐
5. soda	☐	☐	☐	☐	☐
6. ______________	☐	☐	☐	☐	☐

A: Do you ever have candy at the movies?
B: Yes, I sometimes have candy.

3 LISTENING Do you play any sports?

Listen to Stephanie ask Raymond about sports. Check (✓) Raymond's answers.

1. ☐ I play football.
   ☐ I play soccer.
2. ☐ Some friends from school.
   ☐ Some friends from work.
3. ☐ At 6:00 A.M.
   ☐ At 6:00 P.M.
4. ☐ Every day.
   ☐ Every week.
5. ☐ On the weekends.
   ☐ In the afternoons.
6. ☐ At the park.
   ☐ In the yard.

4 SPEAKING My favorite things

A Complete the chart with things you love, like, and don't like.

	I love . . .	**I like . . .**	**I don't like . . .**
Sports			
Other activities			
Foods			
Clothes			

B **PAIR WORK** Find out what your partner loves, likes, and doesn't like. Then ask more questions with *who*, *where*, *how often*, or *when*.

A: What sports do you love?
B: I love bike riding.

A: Who do you usually go bike riding with?
B: I usually go with my brother and sister.

5 SPEAKING Talents and abilities

GROUP WORK What can these people do well? Make a list. Use the abilities in the box and your own ideas. Then tell the class.

chef

mechanic

artist

musician

A: A chef can cook very well.
B: A chef can also bake things, like cakes and cookies.
A: Also, a chef can . . .

bake	fix a motorcycle
cook	paint
draw	play the guitar
fix a car	read music

WHAT'S NEXT?

Look at your Self-assessment again. Do you need to review anything?

11 I'm going to have a party.

- Discuss evening, weekend, and birthday plans
- Discuss plans to celebrate holidays, special occasions, and festivals

1 WORD POWER Months and dates

A Listen and practice the months of the year.

Months					
January	February	March	April	May	June
July	August	September	October	November	December

B Complete the dates. Then listen and practice.

Dates					
1st	first	11th	eleventh	21st	twenty-first
2nd	second		twelfth		twenty-second
	third	13th	thirteenth	23rd	twenty-third
4th	fourth	14th	fourteenth		twenty-fourth
5th	fifth		fifteenth	25th	twenty-fifth
	sixth	16th	sixteenth		twenty-sixth
7th	seventh	17th	seventeenth	27th	twenty-seventh
8th	eighth	18th	eighteenth		twenty-eighth
9th	ninth		nineteenth	29th	twenty-ninth
	tenth	20th	twentieth		thirtieth
					thirty-first

C **CLASS ACTIVITY** Go around the room. Ask for your classmates' birthdays.

A: When's your birthday?
B: It's November eighteenth. When's yours?

2 CONVERSATION Is she going to bake a cake?

Listen and practice.

AVA Are you going to do anything exciting this weekend?

MARTIN Well, I'm going to celebrate my birthday.

AVA Oh, happy birthday! When is it, exactly?

MARTIN It's April twenty-first – Sunday.

AVA So what are your plans?

MARTIN I'm going to go to my friend Rosa's house. She's going to cook a special dinner for me.

AVA Nice! Is Rosa going to bake a birthday cake for you, too?

MARTIN A cake for me? Mmm . . . I hope so!

3 GRAMMAR FOCUS

The future with *be going to*

Are you **going to do** anything this weekend?	Yes, I am. **I'm going to celebrate** my birthday. No, I'm not. **I'm going to stay** home.
Is Rosa **going to cook** dinner for you?	Yes, she is. She**'s going to cook** a special dinner. No, she's not. She**'s going to order** takeout.
Are your friends **going to be** there?	Yes, they are. They**'re going to stop** by after dinner. No, they're not. They**'re going to be** away all weekend.

GRAMMAR PLUS *see page 142*

A What are these people going to do this weekend? Write sentences. Then compare with a partner.

1. *He's going to go biking.*

B **PAIR WORK** Is your partner going to do the things in part A this weekend? Ask and answer questions.

"Are you going to go biking this weekend?"

4 PRONUNCIATION Reduction of *going to*

A Listen and practice. Notice the reduction of **going to** to /gənə/.

A: Are you **going to** go to the game?
B: No. I'm **going to** study for a test.

A: Are you **going to** go to a restaurant?
B: Yes. We're **going to** go to Nick's Café.

B **PAIR WORK** Ask your partner about his or her evening plans. Try to reduce **going to**.

5 LISTENING Holiday plans

A What are these people's plans for a Monday holiday? Write your guesses in the chart.

B Listen to the interview. What are the people really going to do on Monday? Complete the chart.

Morgan Isaac Brian Lauren

	Your guess	What they're really going to do
Morgan	*Morgan is going to go to the gym.*	
Isaac		
Brian		
Lauren		

6 INTERCHANGE 11 Take a guess

Make guesses about your classmates' plans. Go to Interchange 11 on page 125.

7 SNAPSHOT

Listen and practice.

Celebrating Holidays in the U.S.

New Year's Eve | Valentine's Day | Independence Day | Halloween | Thanksgiving | Christmas

Do you celebrate any of these holidays? Do any of your friends celebrate them?
What are some holidays in your country? What's your favorite holiday?

8 CONVERSATION We're going to go dancing.

Listen and practice.

ALLIE So, Jim, do you have any plans for Valentine's Day?

JIM I sure do. I'm going to take Marissa out for dinner.

ALLIE Oh, really? Where are you going to eat?

JIM At the Red Rose. They have great desserts.

ALLIE Wow! That sounds really nice!

JIM Yeah! How about you? What are you and Matt going to do?

ALLIE Well, we're not going to go to a fancy restaurant. We're going to go dancing.

JIM Sounds like fun, too.

9 GRAMMAR FOCUS

Wh-questions with *be going to*

What are you **going to do** for Valentine's Day?	I**'m going to go** to a dance club.
	I**'m not going to go** to a restaurant.
How is Allie **going to get** to the dance club?	She**'s going to drive**.
	She**'s not going to take** the bus.
Where are Jim and his girlfriend **going to eat**?	They**'re going to eat** at the Red Rose.
	They**'re not going to eat** at Nick's Café.

GRAMMAR PLUS see page 142

A Complete these conversations with the correct form of *be going to*. Then practice with a partner.

1. **A:** Where ___are___ you ___going to spend___ (spend) Thanksgiving?
   B: My parents and I ____________ (visit) my grandparents.
2. **A:** Who ____________ you ____________ (invite) to your Independence Day picnic?
   B: I ____________ (ask) my family and some good friends.
3. **A:** What ____________ you ____________ (do) for New Year's Day?
   B: I don't know. I ____________ (not do) anything special.
4. **A:** How ____________ your children ____________ (celebrate) Halloween?
   B: They ____________ (go) to their school's party.
5. **A:** What ____________ your sister ____________ (do) for Valentine's Day?
   B: Her boyfriend ____________ (take) her out to dinner.

B **GROUP WORK** Ask your classmates about their plans. Use the names of holidays and the time expressions in the box.

A: What are you going to do tonight?
B: I'm going to go to a party.
C: Oh, really? Who's going to be there?
B: Well, Chris and Sam are going to come. . . .

time expressions	
tonight	next week
tomorrow	next month
tomorrow afternoon	next summer
tomorrow night	next year

10 WORD POWER Let's celebrate!

A Listen and practice.

wear special clothes

eat special food

decorate

give gifts

play music

go to a parade

go on a picnic

watch fireworks

B **PAIR WORK** Are you going to celebrate a special day this year? Are you (or is someone you know) going to do any of the things in part A?

A: I'm going to go to a wedding next month. I'm going to wear special clothes.
B: Is it a family member's wedding?

11 SPEAKING Holidays and festivals

A **PAIR WORK** Choose any holiday or festival. Then ask and answer these questions.

What is the holiday or festival?
When is it?
What are you going to do?
Where are you going to go?
Who's going to be there?
When are you going to go?
How are you going to get there?

A: What is the holiday or festival?
B: It's my city's Cherry Blossom Festival.
A: When is it?
B: It's on March twenty-third.
A: What are you going to do?
B: I'm going to go to the park. . . .

B **CLASS ACTIVITY** Tell the class about your partner's plans.

Carnival, Brazil

Cherry Blossom Festival, Japan

12 READING

A Scan the blog post. Who sends a letter when people are 100 years old?

Home Posts Archives Follow

HAPPY BIRTHDAY TO YOU!

In this week's blog, we look at some birthday customs around the world.

Harry Baker, Perth, Australia
It's my birthday next Wednesday. I'm going to be 10 years old. In my country, we always eat fairy bread on our birthdays. My mom's going to make me a huge plate of fairy bread. It's a snack. We make it with bread, butter, and colorful sugar called "hundreds and thousands."

Jim Dixon, Montego Bay, Jamaica
I love birthdays! They're a lot of fun. Here in Jamaica, we have an old custom. We like to surprise people on their birthday. Guess what we do? We throw flour at our friends! It's my best friend's birthday tomorrow. I'm going to go to the store soon. I'm going to buy a lot of flour to throw at him.

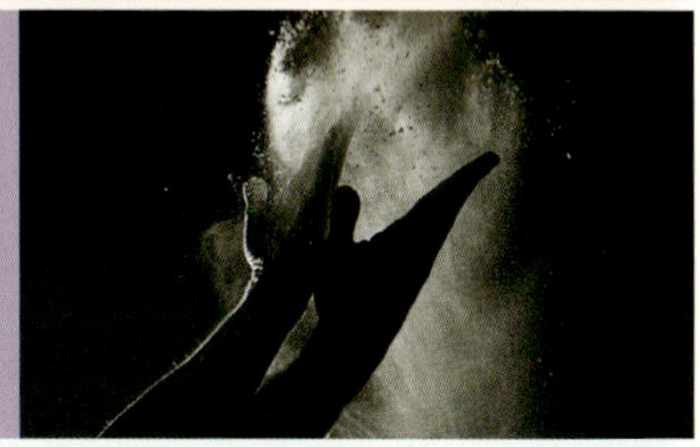

Victoria Smith, London, UK
My grandmother is going to be 100 years old in June. She's very excited because she's going to get a special letter from the Queen. The Queen sends a letter to every person who reaches 100. It's a tradition that makes people very happy.

Jiang Li, Beijing, China
In my country, we celebrate birthdays with a special type of food. Noodles are a sign of long life for us. This year, I'm going to make some "long life noodles" for all my friends. We're going to eat them together and have a great evening!

B Read the questions. Write short answers.

1. Which two countries celebrate birthdays with food? ____________
2. Why is Jim going to the store? ____________
3. What three things do you need to make fairy bread? ____________
4. What do noodles mean in China? ____________

C **GROUP WORK** How do people usually celebrate birthdays in your country? Do you have plans for your next birthday? How about the birthday of a friend or a family member? What are you going to do? Tell your classmates.

12 How do you feel?

▸ Discuss the body and common ailments
▸ Discuss common remedies and give health advice

1 WORD POWER Parts of the body

A Listen and practice.

B **GROUP WORK** Say a sentence with a body part. Take turns repeating the sentence and keep adding body parts. The group with the last student to say a correct sentence wins.

A: I have one head.
B: I have one head and two eyes.
C: I have one head, two eyes, and one nose.
D: I have one head, two eyes, one nose, and . . .

2 CONVERSATION Do you want some tea?

Listen and practice.

Craig: Hi, Nathan. How's it going?
Nathan: Oh, hi, Craig. Not so well, actually. I don't feel well.
Craig: Yeah, you don't look so good. What's wrong?
Nathan: I don't know. I have a stomachache.
Craig: That's too bad. Do you have the flu?
Nathan: No, I just feel really sick.
Craig: Well, can I get you anything? Do you want some tea?
Nathan: No, but thanks anyway.
Craig: Well, I'm going to have some pizza. Is that OK? Call me if you need me.

3 GRAMMAR FOCUS

Have + noun; *feel* + adjective

		Negative adjectives	Positive adjectives
What's the matter?	How are you?	horrible	fine
What's wrong?	How do you feel?	awful	great
I have a stomachache.	**I feel sick.**	terrible	terrific
I have a headache.	**I feel better.**	miserable	fantastic
I have the flu.	**I don't feel well.**		

GRAMMAR PLUS *see page 143*

A Listen and practice. *"He has a backache."*

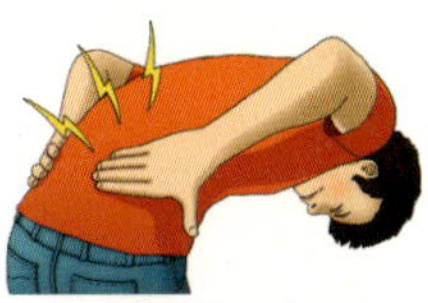
a backache

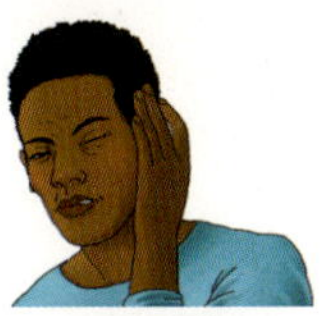
an earache

a headache

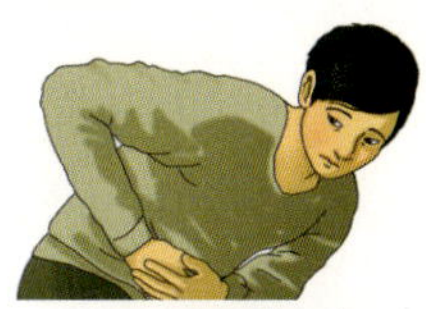
a stomachache

a toothache

a cold

a cough

a fever

the flu

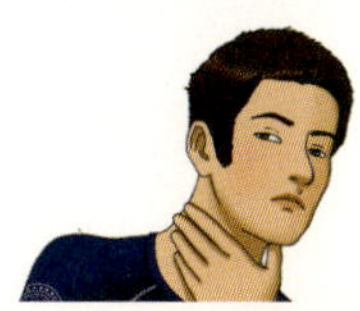
a sore throat

B **CLASS ACTIVITY** Imagine you don't feel well today. Go around the class. Find out what's wrong with your classmates.

A: How are you today, Paul?
B: I feel terrible. I have a backache.
A: I'm sorry to hear that.
B: How do *you* feel?

useful expressions

That's good.
I'm glad to hear that.
That's too bad.
I'm sorry to hear that.

4 LISTENING Are you OK?

A Where do these people hurt? Guess. Write down the parts of the body.

1. Amber ______________________

2. David ______________________

3. Alyssa ______________________

4. Nicholas ______________________

B Listen to the conversations. Check your guesses.

5 SNAPSHOT

Listen and practice.

Common Remedies

What medications or home remedies do you use when you're sick?
What remedies are good, in your opinion? What remedies aren't good?

6 CONVERSATION Try to relax.

Listen and practice.

Dr. Yun Hello, Ms. Lake. How are you today?

Ms. Lake Not so good.

Dr. Yun What's wrong, exactly?

Ms. Lake I'm exhausted!

Dr. Yun Hmm. Why are you so tired?

Ms. Lake I don't know. I just can't sleep at night.

Dr. Yun OK. Let's take a look at you.

A few minutes later . . .

Dr. Yun I'm going to give you some pills. Take one pill every evening after dinner.

Ms. Lake OK.

Dr. Yun And don't drink coffee, tea, or soda.

Ms. Lake Anything else?

Dr. Yun Yes. Try to relax.

Ms. Lake All right. Thanks, Dr. Yun.

7 LISTENING I think I have a cold.

Listen to Dr. Yun talk to four other patients. What does she give them? Check (✓) the correct medications.

	Cough syrup	Aspirin	Cold medicine	Eye drops	Nasal spray	Ice packs
1. Roberto	☐	☐	☐	☐	☐	☐
2. Courtney	☐	☐	☐	☐	☐	☐
3. Ryan	☐	☐	☐	☐	☐	☐
4. Samantha	☐	☐	☐	☐	☐	☐

8 PRONUNCIATION Sentence intonation

A Listen and practice. Notice the intonation in these sentences.

Take these pills. Don't take cough syrup.

Drink some tea. Don't drink coffee.

Try to relax. Don't work too hard.

B PAIRWORK Practice the conversation in Exercise 6 again. Pay attention to the sentence intonation.

9 GRAMMAR FOCUS

Imperatives

Get some rest.	**Don't stay** up late.
Drink lots of juice.	**Don't drink** soda.
Take one pill every evening.	**Don't work** too hard.

GRAMMAR PLUS *see page 143*

Complete these sentences. Use the correct forms of the words in the box.

✓call	stay	not go	not drink
see	take	✓not worry	not eat

1. Call a dentist.
2. Don't worry too much.
3. ______ a hot bath.
4. ______ to school.
5. ______ in bed.
6. ______ a doctor.
7. ______ coffee.
8. ______ any candy.

10 SPEAKING Good advice?

A Write two pieces of advice for each problem.

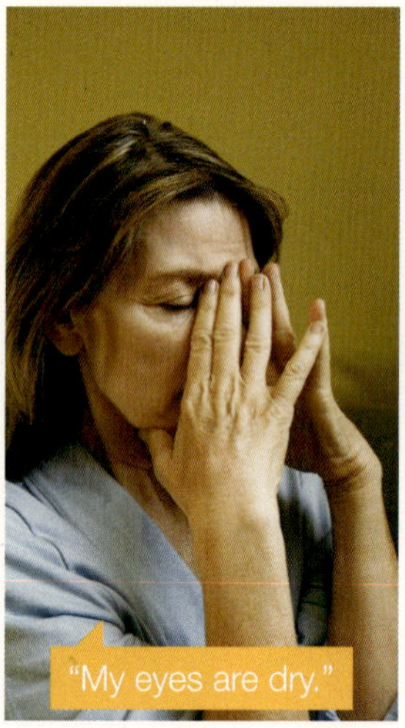

1. ______
2. ______
3. ______
4. ______

B **GROUP WORK** Act out the problems from part A. Your classmates give advice.

A: I don't feel well.
B: What's the matter?

A: My feet hurt.
B: I have an idea. Take a hot bath. And don't . . .

11 INTERCHANGE 12 Problems, problems

Give advice for common problems. Go to Interchange 12 on page 126.

12 READING

A What does your body do to keep you alive? Take the quiz to find out!

DO YOU KNOW YOUR BODY?

1. The human heart beats about 200 times a minute.
   - [ ] True - [ ] False
2. Your body loses about 40,000 tiny pieces of skin an hour.
   - [ ] True - [ ] False
3. Your brain sends billions of signals every minute.
   - [ ] True - [ ] False
4. Your brain stops working when you're asleep.
   - [ ] True - [ ] False
5. 140 million cells in your eyes help to tell you what you can see.
   - [ ] True - [ ] False
6. Brain cells do not live in the stomach.
   - [ ] True - [ ] False
7. Women's hearts beat faster than men's hearts.
   - [ ] True - [ ] False
8. Your brain makes electricity.
   - [ ] True - [ ] False
9. Your natural smell changes as you age.
   - [ ] True - [ ] False
10. Some bacteria (small living things) in your body help you live.
    - [ ] True - [ ] False

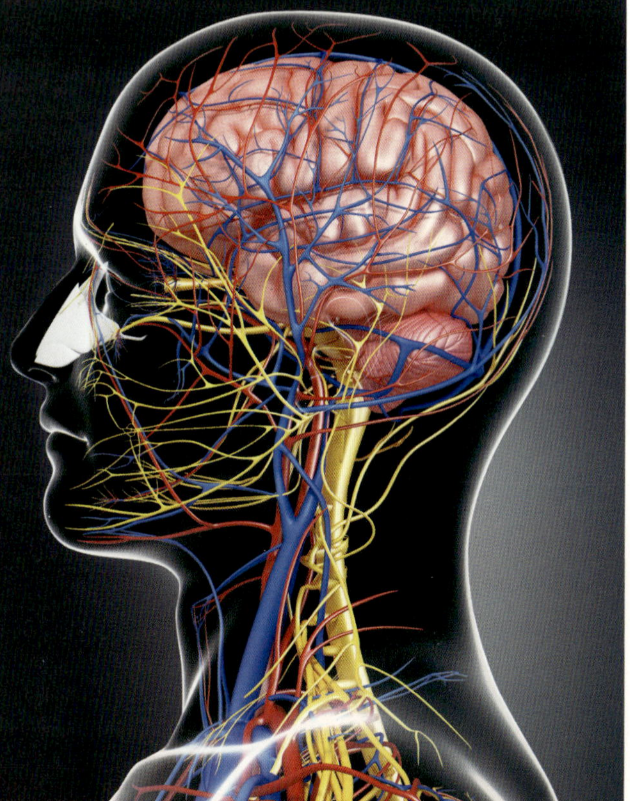

1. False 2. True 3. True 4. False 5. True 6. False 7. True 8. True 9. True 10. True

B Read and answer the quiz. Check your answers. Then answer the questions.

1. What does your body lose every hour? ______________________
2. What part of the body sends signals and makes electricity? ______________________
3. What is one thing that changes as you age? ______________________
4. What cells live in the stomach? ______________________
5. What's another name for small living things? ______________________

C **GROUP WORK** What information in the quiz is most surprising? What else do you know about the human body? Tell your classmates.

Units 11–12 Progress check

SELF-ASSESSMENT

How well can you do these things? Check (✓) the boxes.

I can . . .	Very well	OK	A little
Talk about ways to celebrate holidays (Ex. 1)	☐	☐	☐
Use future time expressions (Ex. 1, 2)	☐	☐	☐
Understand conversations about problems (Ex. 3)	☐	☐	☐
Talk about problems (Ex. 4)	☐	☐	☐
Ask how people are and give advice (Ex. 4)	☐	☐	☐

1 SPEAKING Holiday customs

A Complete the questions with names of different holidays.

Are you going to . . . ?	Name
eat special food on	
give gifts on	
have a party on	
play music on	
wear special clothes on	

B CLASS ACTIVITY Are your classmates going to do the things in part A? Go around the class and find out. Try to write a different person's name on each line.

2 SPEAKING Future plans

Complete these questions with different time expressions. Add one more question. Then ask a partner the questions.

1. How are you going to get home tonight?
2. What time are you going to go to bed ______________?
3. Where are you going to go ______________?
4. What are you going to do ______________?
5. Who are you going to eat dinner with ______________?
6. ____?

3 LISTENING Everyone has problems.

Listen to six conversations. Number the pictures from 1 to 6.

☐ This person can't dance very well.

☐ This person has the flu.

☐ This person needs some ketchup.

☐ This person has a backache.

☐ This person doesn't want to go to the dentist.

[1] This person feels sad.

4 SPEAKING Thanks for the advice!

A Write a problem on a piece of paper. Then write advice for the problem on a different piece of paper.

I have a toothache.

Call your dentist.

B **CLASS ACTIVITY** Put the papers with problems and the papers with advice in two different boxes. Then take a new paper from each box. Go around the class and find the right advice for your problem.

A: I feel terrible.
B: What's the matter?
A: I have a toothache.
B: I can help. Drink some tea.
A: Er . . . I don't know. But thanks, anyway.

A: I feel awful.
C: Why? What's wrong?
A: I have a toothache.
C: I know! Call your dentist.
A: That's great advice. Thanks!

WHAT'S NEXT?

Look at your Self-assessment again. Do you need to review anything?

13 How do I get there?

- Discuss stores, their locations, and things to buy there
- Ask for and give directions to various locations

1 WORD POWER Places to go, things to buy

A Where can you get these things? Match the things with the places. Then listen and practice.

"You can buy a backpack at a department store."

a. a post office

b. a drugstore

c. a gas station

1. a backpack ___d___
2. cold medicine _____
3. a debit card _____
4. eggs _____
5. an espresso _____
6. gasoline _____
7. a magazine _____
8. stamps _____

d. a department store

e. a bank

f. a bookstore

g. a coffee shop

h. a supermarket

B PAIR WORK What else can you get or do in the places in part A?

A: You can send packages at a post office.

B: And you get cereal and milk at a supermarket.

2 LISTENING I can't find my cell phone.

A Vanessa is looking for her cell phone with her friend Tom. What does Tom need? Where is he going to get the things? Complete the chart.

	What does Tom need?	Where is he going to get it?
1.		
2.		
3.		
4.		

B **PAIR WORK** What do you need? Where are you going to get it? Tell your partner.

"I need some gas, so I'm going to go to the gas station. . . ."

3 CONVERSATION Excuse me. Can you help me?

Listen and practice.

Mother: Excuse me. Can you help me? Is there a public restroom around here?

Passer-by: A public restroom? Hmm. I'm sorry. I don't think so.

Mother: Oh, no. My son needs a restroom – now. It's an emergency!

Passer-by: Hmm . . . Let's see . . . Oh, there's a restroom in the department store on Third Avenue.

Mother: Where on Third Avenue?

Passer-by: It's on the corner of Third Avenue and Market Street.

Mother: On the corner of Third and Market?

Passer-by: Yes, it's across from the park. You can't miss it.

Mother: Thanks a lot.

4 PRONUNCIATION Compound nouns

A Listen and practice. Notice the stress in these compound nouns.

bookstore	department store	gas station	post office
coffee shop	drugstore	restroom	supermarket

B **PAIR WORK** Practice these sentences. Pay attention to the stress in the compound nouns.

There's a bookstore in the gas station.
There's a coffee shop in the supermarket.
There isn't a post office in the supermarket.
There aren't restrooms in the drugstore.

5 GRAMMAR FOCUS

Prepositions of place

on

on the corner of

across from

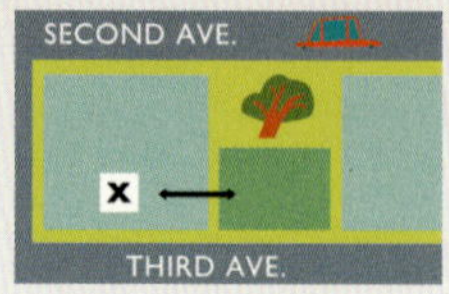

next to

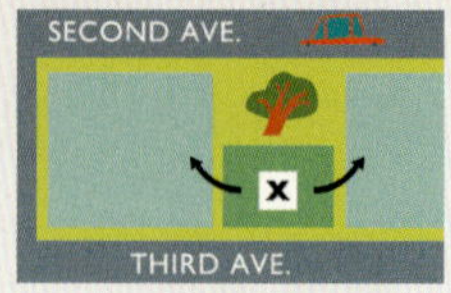

between

The department store is **on** Third Avenue.
It's **on the corner of** Third and Market.
It's **across from** the park.

It's **next to** the bank.
The bank is **between** the department store **and** the restaurant.

GRAMMAR PLUS see page 144

A Look at the map and complete the sentences. Then compare with a partner.

1. The coffee shop is ___*on*___ Main Street. It's ____________ the shoe store.
2. The movie theater is ____________ Park and Third. It's ____________ the park.
3. The gas station is ____________ the parking lot. It's ____________ Second and Market.
4. The post office is ____________ Main and Second. It's ____________ the hospital.
5. The bank is ____________ the restaurant and the department store.
   It's ____________ Third Avenue.

B **PAIR WORK** Where are these places on the map? Ask and answer questions.

the park **the drugstore** **the bookstore** **the hospital** **the shoe store**

A: Where is the park?
B: It's between Park and Market, across from the department store.

6 LISTENING I think it's on Main Street.

Look at the map in Exercise 5. Listen to four conversations. Where are the people going? Number the places from 1 to 4.

☐ the hospital ☐ the bank ☐ the gas station ☐ the coffee shop

7 SNAPSHOT

Listen and practice.

NEW YORK CITY'S Tourist Attractions

The Empire State Building

Brooklyn Bridge

Central Park

Times Square

Rockefeller Center

The Statue of Liberty

What do you know about these places? What makes them popular?
What are some popular tourist attractions in your country? What are your top five attractions?

8 CONVERSATION How do I get to Rockefeller Center?

Listen and practice.

Tourist: Excuse me, sir. Can you help me? How do I get to Rockefeller Center?

Man: Just walk up Sixth Avenue to 49th Street. Rockefeller Center is on the right.

Tourist: Is it near Radio City Music Hall?

Man: Yes, it's right across from Radio City Music Hall.

Tourist: Thank you. And where is the Empire State Building? Is it far from here?

Man: It's right behind you. Just turn around and look up!

9 GRAMMAR FOCUS

Directions

How do I get to Rockefeller Center?	**How can I get to** the New York Public Library?
Walk up/Go up Fifth Avenue.	**Walk down/Go down** Fifth Avenue.
Turn left on 49th Street.	**Turn right on** 42nd Street.
It's **on the right**.	It's **on the left**.

GRAMMAR PLUS see page 144

A PAIR WORK Imagine you are tourists at Grand Central Terminal. Ask for directions. Follow the arrows.

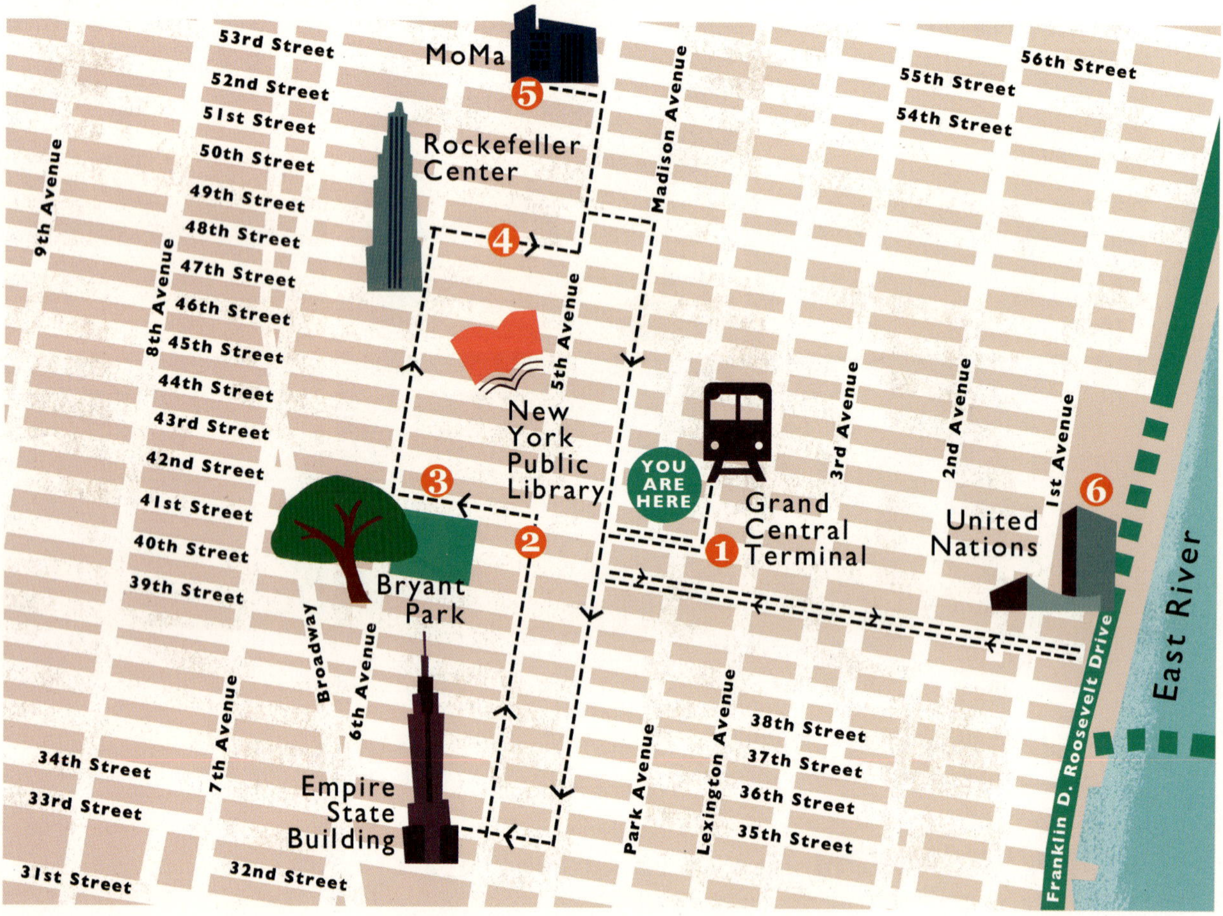

A: Excuse me. How do I get to the Empire State Building?
B: Walk up 42nd Street. Turn left on . . .

B PAIR WORK Ask for directions to places near your school.

A: How do I get to the bus stop?
B: Walk . . .

10 INTERCHANGE 13 Giving directions

Student A, go to Interchange 13A on page 127; Student B, go to Interchange 13B on page 128.

11 READING

A Skim the guide. Where can you have some tea?

A Tour of Palermo, Buenos Aires

1 The art museum

Why not start at MALBA, the art museum on Avenida Figuero Alcorta? There are some fantastic sculptures and paintings there.

2 Japanese Gardens

Next, walk up to the park, turn left, and get a taste of Japan in Argentina. You can visit the Japanese Gardens and see about 150 different types of plants from Japan. Don't forget to taste some Japanese tea before you leave.

3 Galileo Galilei planetarium

Then turn right on Avenida Sarmiento and head over to the Galileo Galilei planetarium. There, you can see a piece of rock from the moon. There's a telescope you can look at the sky through, too.

4 The Spanish Monument

Across the park from the planetarium, you can see the Spanish Monument. It's a huge statue. It's a gift from the Spanish people to the Argentinian people.

5 Statue of Domingo Faustino Sarmiento

Turn right to see another big statue. That's the statue of Domingo Faustino Sarmiento. He was a writer and a president of Argentina. Auguste Rodin, a famous French artist, made the statue.

6 Campo Argentino del Polo

End your tour at the Campo Argentino del Polo. That's where people play a sport named polo, on horseback. The biggest polo competition in the world takes place there!

B Read the information in the guide. Where can you . . . ?

1. see horses ______________
2. look at the sky ______________
3. see many types of plants ______________
4. find a statue of a writer ______________
5. see some art ______________

C **PAIR WORK** Think of a place you both know and like. Plan a guide to tell visitors where things are.

14 I had a good time.

- Discuss past weekend activities
- Discuss past vacation activities

1 SNAPSHOT

Listen and practice.

THINGS TO DO ON THE WEEKEND

Check (✓) the activities you usually do on weekends. Do you like doing them? Why or why not? What other activities do you do on the weekends?

2 CONVERSATION Did you have a good weekend?

Listen and practice.

Shaun: Hi, Yuna. Did you have a good weekend?

Yuna: Well, I had a busy weekend, so I'm a little tired.

Shaun: Really? Why?

Yuna: Well, on Saturday, I exercised in the morning. Then I cleaned the apartment, did the laundry, and went shopping. And in the evening, I visited my parents.

Shaun: And what did you do on Sunday?

Yuna: I studied for our test all day.

Shaun: Oh, no! I didn't study for the test! I just watched TV shows all weekend!

3 GRAMMAR FOCUS

Simple past statements; regular verbs

I	**stayed**	home.	I	**didn't stay**	home.
You	**watched**	a TV show.	You	**didn't watch**	a game.
She	**exercised**	on Saturday.	She	**didn't exercise**	on Sunday.
We	**studied**	English.	We	**didn't study**	math.
They	**shopped**	for groceries.	They	**didn't shop**	for clothes.

did**n't** = did **not**

Spelling

stay	→	stay**ed**
watch	→	watch**ed**
exercise	→	exercise**d**
study	→	stud**ied**
shop	→	shop**ped**

GRAMMAR PLUS *see page 145*

A Ray is talking about his weekend. Complete the sentences. Then compare with a partner.

On Friday night, I ___wanted___ (want) to go out, but my friends ______________ (not call). I ______________ (decide) to stay home, and I ______________ (play) video games. On Saturday, I ______________ (visit) my friend Pablo. We ______________ (talk) and ______________ (listen) to music. In the evening, he ______________ (invite) some friends over, and we ______________ (cook) a great meal. I ______________ (not work) very hard on Sunday. I ______________ (not study) at all. I just ______________ (walk) to the mall and ______________ (shop).

B Complete the sentences. Use your own information. Then compare with a partner.

1. Yesterday, I ______________ (watch) a basketball game.
2. Last night, I ______________ (stay) home.
3. Last week, I ______________ (clean) the house.
4. Last month, I ______________ (shop) for clothes.
5. Last year, I ______________ (visit) a different country.

4 PRONUNCIATION Simple past *–ed* endings.

A Listen and practice. Notice the pronunciation of –**ed**.

/t/	/d/	/ɪd/
worked	cleaned	wanted
watched	stayed	visited

B Listen and write these verbs under the correct sounds.

cooked **decided** **exercised** **invited** **listened** **shopped**

5 GRAMMAR FOCUS

Simple past statements: irregular verbs

I **did** my homework.
I **didn't do** the laundry.

You **got up** at noon.
You **didn't get up** at 8:00.

She **went** to the bookstore.
She **didn't go** to the library.

We **met** our classmates.
We **didn't meet** our teacher.

You **came** home late.
You **didn't come** home early.

They **had** a barbecue.
They **didn't have** a picnic.

GRAMMAR PLUS *see page 145*

A Complete the chart. Then listen and check.

Present	Past	Present	Past	Present	Past
________	bought	________	made	________	saw
________	ate	________	read /rɛd/	________	sat
________	felt	________	rode	________	took

B **PAIR WORK** Did you do the things in the pictures yesterday? Tell your partner.

"Yesterday, I didn't do my homework. But I did the laundry. . . ."

6 SPEAKING Last weekend

A Write five things you did and five things you didn't do last weekend.

Things I did	Things I didn't do
I went to a party.	I didn't clean the house.
I danced a lot.	I didn't see a movie.
I . . .	I didn't . . .

B **GROUP WORK** Tell your classmates about your weekend.

A: I went to a party last weekend.
B: I didn't go to a party. But I met my friends.
C: I met my friends, too! We went . . .

7 CONVERSATION Did you have fun?

Listen and practice.

KIM Hi, Martin! Welcome back! So, did you go to Montreal?

MARTIN No, I didn't. I went to Sydney with my sister.

KIM Really? Did you like it?

MARTIN Yeah, we loved it! We visited the Opera House and went to Bondi Beach.

KIM Did you go surfing?

MARTIN No, we didn't. Actually, we went swimming in the Ocean Pool. And one day we climbed Sydney Harbor Bridge.

KIM Wow! Did you have fun?

MARTIN Yes, I did. But my sister didn't like climbing very much. She got really tired.

8 GRAMMAR FOCUS

Simple past yes/no questions

Did you **have** a good summer?
Yes, I **did**. I **had** a great summer.
Did you **go** surfing?
No, I **didn't**. I **went** swimming.

Did Martin **like** his vacation?
Yes, he **did**. He **liked** it a lot.
Did Martin and his sister **go** to Montreal?
No, they **didn't**. They **went** to Sydney.

GRAMMAR PLUS *see page 145*

A Complete the conversations. Then practice with a partner.

1. **A:** ___Did___ you ___have___ (have) a good summer?
   B: Yes, I __________. I __________ (have) a great summer.
   I __________ (go) out with my friends a lot.
2. **A:** __________ you __________ (go) anywhere last summer?
   B: No, I __________. I __________ (stay) here.
   I __________ (get) a part-time job, so I __________ (make) some extra money.
3. **A:** __________ you __________ (take) any classes last summer?
   B: Yes, I __________. I __________ (take) tennis lessons, and
   I __________ (play) tennis every day!
4. **A:** __________ you __________ (speak) English last summer?
   B: No, I __________. But I __________ (read) blogs
   in English, and I __________ (watch) English movies.

B **PAIR WORK** Ask the questions from part A. Answer with your own information.

A: Did you have a good summer?
B: Yes, I did. I went to the beach every day.

9 LISTENING Did you have a good summer?

Listen to Fernando, Olivia, Cameron, and Abigail. What did they do last summer? Check (✓) the correct answers.

Fernando	Olivia	Cameron	Abigail
☐ stayed home	☐ watched videos	☐ went bike riding	☐ worked in the yard
☐ visited his brother	☐ read books	☐ went swimming	☐ got a job
☐ went to the beach	☐ watched TV	☐ played baseball	☐ painted the house

10 WORD POWER Summer activities

A Find two words from the list that go with each verb in the chart. Then listen and check.

a barbecue	a picnic
beach volleyball	soccer
camping	a summer class
✓a new bike	swimming
new people	a trip
old friends	✓ up late

get	a new bike	up late
go		
have		
meet		
play		
take		

B **PAIR WORK** Add two activities to the list. Check (✓) six things to ask your partner. Then ask and answer questions.

Did you . . . last summer?

☐ do anything interesting	☐ play any games
☐ eat any new foods	☐ read any books
☐ see any museum exhibits	☐ see any movies
☐ meet any interesting people	☐ take any classes
☐ play any sports	☐ take any trips
☐ ______________	☐ ______________

A: Did you do anything interesting last summer?
B: Yes, I did. I went white-water rafting.

C **CLASS ACTIVITY** Tell the class about your partner's summer.

"Last summer, Alma went white-water rafting with some friends. They had a lot of fun."

11 INTERCHANGE 14 Past activities

Did you and your partner do similar things when you were children? Go to Interchange 14 on page 129.

12 READING

A Scan the social media posts. Who had a busy weekend? Who saw old friends on the weekend? Who had fun learning something new? Who had a terrible weekend?

SOCIAL Find friends

DID YOU HAVE A GOOD WEEKEND?

Nick Bond

I just had the worst weekend ever! It was my best friend Pete's wedding and my car broke down on the drive. I was on a quiet road and suddenly there was a bang. Then the car just didn't move! I missed the wedding and came home on the back of a truck. ☹

like comment Share post

Jessie Taylor

Hey guys! Guess what? I just got back from my first ever parasailing class! It was amazing! I traveled to a town by the ocean and met my instructor. We went high up above the ocean where people jump off the rocks. It was kind of scary but so exciting. Here's a picture of me. See? That's me!

like comment Share post

Armando Torres

So . . . on Saturday morning I did chores at home. You know, laundry and stuff. Then I went grocery shopping because . . . well, because there was no food in the house! Sunday morning, I fixed my bike, walked the dog, called my mom, and made lunch. Then I wrote a report for work, cleaned the house, and went to bed.

like comment Share post

Juliette Blum

Wow. What an awesome weekend. I went running in the park on Saturday evening, and I met someone I knew from school 10 years ago. It was so cool. Her name is Marie and we always hung out together when we were kids. She's married now and has a baby!

like comment Share post

B Read the social media posts. Then correct these sentences.

1. Nick got married. *Nick's best friend got married.*
2. On the way to the wedding, Nick's truck broke down. ______
3. Jessie's parasailing class was terrible. ______
4. It was Jessie's second parasailing class. ______
5. Armando watched TV on Saturday morning. ______
6. Armando fixed his car and walked his dog. ______
7. Juliette went running on Sunday morning. ______
8. Juliette is married and has a baby. ______

C **PAIR WORK** How was your weekend? Did you have fun? Why? Why not? Tell your partner.

Units 13–14 Progress check

SELF-ASSESSMENT

How well can you do these things? Check (✓) the boxes.

I can . . .	Very well	OK	A little
Understand conversations about where to get things in a town (Ex. 1)	☐	☐	☐
Ask and answer questions about where places are (Ex. 2)	☐	☐	☐
Ask for and give directions (Ex. 2)	☐	☐	☐
Talk about past activities (Ex. 3, 4)	☐	☐	☐
Ask and answer questions about past activities (Ex. 4)	☐	☐	☐

1 LISTENING What are you looking for?

Listen to the conversations. What do the people need?
Where can they get or find it? Complete the chart.

What?	Where?
1.	
2.	
3.	
4.	

2 SPEAKING Is there a . . . near here?

A **PAIR WORK** Are these places near your school? Where are they? Ask and answer questions.

bank	coffee shop	hospital	post office
bookstore	department store	park	supermarket

A: Is there a bank near here?
B: Yes, there's a bank on Second Avenue. It's across from the Korean restaurant.

B **PAIR WORK** Give directions from your school to the places in part A. Your partner guesses the place.

A: Go out of the school and turn left. Walk for about three minutes. It's on the right, next to the drugstore.
B: It's the coffee shop.
A: That's right!

3 SPEAKING On my last vacation . . .

A Write four statements about your last vacation. Two are true and two are false.

B **PAIR WORK** Read your statements. Your partner says, "I think it's true," OR "I think it's false." Who has more correct guesses?

I went to New Zealand.
It rained all day, every day.
I didn't go to the beach.
I read two books.

A: On my last vacation, I went to New Zealand.
B: I think it's false.
A: That's right. It's false. OR Sorry. It's true.

4 SPEAKING Did you . . . last weekend?

A Check (✓) the things you did last weekend. Then add two more things you did.

Last weekend, I . . .

- ☐ ate at a restaurant
- ☐ cleaned the house
- ☐ did homework
- ☐ did the laundry
- ☐ downloaded movies
- ☐ exercised
- ☐ played video games
- ☐ rode my bicycle
- ☐ visited relatives
- ☐ washed the car
- ☐ watched a game on TV
- ☐ uploaded photos
- ☐ went shopping
- ☐ went out with friends
- ☐ ____________
- ☐ ____________

B **PAIR WORK** Ask your partner about his or her weekend.

A: Did you eat at a restaurant last weekend, Narumi?
B: Yes, I did. I ate at a very good Italian restaurant. What about you? Did you eat at a restaurant?
A: No, I didn't. . . .

C **GROUP WORK** Join another pair. Tell them about your partner's weekend.

"Narumi ate at a very good Italian restaurant."

WHAT'S NEXT?

Look at your Self-assessment again. Do you need to review anything?

15 Where were you born?

▸ Discuss family and personal history
▸ Discuss school experiences and memories

1 SNAPSHOT

Listen and practice.

Where Were They Born?

Esperanza Spalding
musician

John Oliver
comedian

Lupita Nyong'o
actress

Shin-Soo Choo
baseball player

Shigeru Miyamoto
game designer

1. ________ 2. ________ 3. ________ 4. ________ 5. ________

a. Japan
b. Mexico
c. South Korea
d. the U.K.
e. the U.S.

Answers: 1. e 2. d 3. b 4. c 5. a

Match the people with the countries where they were born. Then check your answers.
What famous people were born in your country? What do they do?

2 CONVERSATION I was born in Brazil.

Listen and practice.

Mario Bianca. That's a nice name. Where were you born?

Bianca I was born in Brazil.

Mario Oh! So you weren't born in the U.S. Your English is really good.

Bianca Thanks. I studied English for many years.

Mario Did you study English in Brazil?

Bianca Yeah, I started when I was seven.

Mario You were pretty young.

Bianca Yes, I went to a bilingual school. I had classes in English and in Portuguese.

Mario You were lucky to learn another language so well.

Bianca Do you speak a second language, too?

Mario Well, I speak a little Italian. My parents were born in Milan.

3 GRAMMAR FOCUS

Past of *be*

I **was** born here.	I **wasn't** born in Italy.	**Were** you in class yesterday?
You **were** pretty young.	You **weren't** very old.	Yes, I **was**. / No, I **wasn't**.
She **was** seven.	She **wasn't** in college.	**Was** your first teacher American?
We **were** at the hair salon.	We **weren't** at the café.	Yes, she **was**. / No, she **wasn't**.
They **were** born in Milan.	They **weren't** born in Rome.	**Were** your parents born in the U.S.?
		Yes, they **were**. / No, they **weren't**.
were**n't** = were **not**	was**n't** = was **not**	

GRAMMAR PLUS *see page 146*

A Bianca is talking about her family. Choose the correct verb forms. Then compare with a partner.

My family and I ___*were*___ (was / were) all born in Brazil – we ____________ (wasn't / weren't) born in the U.S. I ____________ (was / were) born in the city of Recife, and my brother ____________ (was / were) born there, too. My parents ____________ (wasn't / weren't) born in Recife. They ____________ (was / were) born in Rio de Janeiro. In Rio, my father ____________ (was / were) a teacher and my mother ____________ (was / were) an engineer. They have their own business in Recife now.

B **PAIR WORK** Look at the picture below. Ask and answer these questions.

1. Was Tessa on time for class yesterday?
2. Was it English class?
3. Was it a sunny day?
4. Was it 10:00?
5. Was Mr. Walker very angry?
6. Were Alyssa and Jacob late to class?
7. Were they at the board?
8. Were the windows open?

A: Was Tessa on time for class yesterday?
B: No, she wasn't. She was late. Was it English class?

4 PRONUNCIATION Negative contractions

A Listen and practice.

one syllable		two syllables	
aren't	don't	isn't	doesn't
weren't	can't	wasn't	didn't

B Listen and practice.

They **didn't** like the comedy because it **wasn't** funny.
I **don't** like coffee, and she **doesn't** like tea.
This **isn't** my book. I **can't** read French.
They **weren't** in class yesterday, and they **aren't** in class today.

C Write four sentences with negative contractions. Then read them to a partner.

I didn't go to the party because my friends weren't there.

5 CONVERSATION I grew up in New York.

Listen and practice.

Bianca So, Mario, where did you grow up?
Mario I grew up in New York.
Bianca Were you born there?
Mario Yeah. I was born in Brooklyn.
Bianca And when did you come to Los Angeles?
Mario In 2008.
Bianca How old were you then?
Mario I was eighteen. I went to college here.
Bianca Oh. What was your major?
Mario Photography. I was a photographer for five years after college.
Bianca Really? Why did you become a hairstylist?
Mario Because I needed the money. And I love it. So, what do you think?
Bianca Well, uh . . .

6 GRAMMAR FOCUS

Wh-questions with *did, was,* and *were*

Where **did** you **grow up**?	I **grew up** in New York.
What **did** your father **do** there?	He **worked** in a department store.
When **did** you **come** to Los Angeles?	I **came** to Los Angeles in 2008.
Why **did** you **become** a hairstylist?	Because I **needed** the money.
Where **were** you **born**?	I **was born** in Brooklyn.
When **were** you **born**?	I **was born** in 1990.
How old **were** you in 2008?	I **was** eighteen.
What **was** your major in college?	Photography. I **was** a photographer for five years.

GRAMMAR PLUS see page 146

A Match the questions with the answers. Then compare with a partner.

1. Where were you born? _e_
2. Where did you grow up? ____
3. How was your first day of school? ____
4. Who was your best friend in school? ____
5. What was he like? ____
6. Why did you take this class? ____

a. His name was Akio.
b. He was really friendly.
c. I wanted to improve my English.
d. I grew up in Tokyo.
e. In Kyoto, Japan.
f. It was a little scary.

B **PAIR WORK** Ask and answer the questions in part A. Use your own information and make the necessary changes.

C **GROUP WORK** Ask the questions. Use a year in your answers.

1. When were you born?
2. When was your father born?
3. When was your mother born?
4. When did you turn 13?
5. When did you start high school?
6. When did you begin to study English?

saying years

1900 = nineteen hundred
1906 = nineteen oh six
1995 = nineteen ninety-five
2000 = two thousand
2007 = two thousand (and) seven
2015 = two thousand (and) fifteen OR twenty-fifteen

7 LISTENING I wasn't born here.

A Listen. What year were these people born? Complete the sentences.

1. Melissa was born in ____________.
2. Colin was born in ____________.
3. Kumiko was born in ____________.
4. Omar was born in ____________.

B Listen again. Where did these people grow up? Complete the sentences.

1. Melissa grew up in ____________.
2. Colin grew up in ____________.
3. Kumiko grew up in ____________.
4. Omar grew up in ____________.

8 WORD POWER School days

A Complete the word map with words from the list. Then listen and check.

✓ auditorium
cafeteria
college
computer lab
elementary school
geography
high school
history
library
middle school
physical education
science

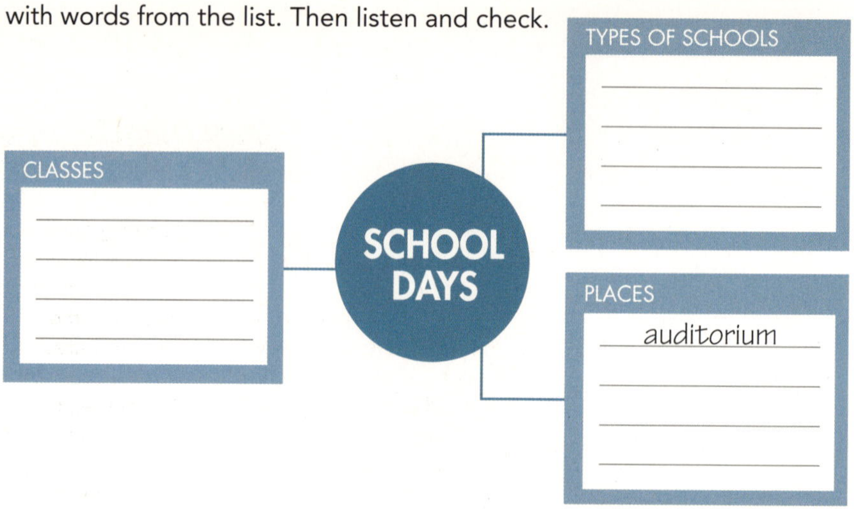

B **PAIR WORK** Find out about your partner's elementary, middle, or high school days. Ask these questions. Then tell the class.

What classes did you take?	Who was your favorite teacher? Why?
What was your favorite class? Why?	Where did you spend your free time? Why?
What classes didn't you like? Why not?	What was a typical day of school like?
Who was your best friend?	What didn't you like about school?

"In high school, Julian's favorite class was physical education because he liked to play sports . . ."

9 SPEAKING Can you remember . . . ?

A **GROUP WORK** How often do you have English class? What do you remember from your last class? Ask and answer these questions.

1. Who was in class? Who wasn't there?
2. Who was late that day?
3. Who was very tired?
4. What color were your teacher's shoes?
5. What were your teacher's first words?
6. Did all the students bring their books?
7. What did you learn?
8. What did you do after class?

B **CLASS ACTIVITY** What does your group remember? Tell the class.

10 INTERCHANGE 15 This is your life.

Did you and your partner do similar things when you were children? Go to Interchange 15 on page 130.

11 READING

A Scan the article. What is a "third culture kid?" Do you know anyone who moved to another country?

THE STORY OF A THIRD CULTURE KID

Tommy was born in Colombo, the largest city in the island country of Sri Lanka. The streets of Colombo were busy, and Tommy loved the colors, sights, and smells. He played on sandy beaches with his friends. He spoke Sinhalese with his friends and family and learned English at school. He loved visiting the neighborhood markets with his family to buy fresh fruits and vegetables. Typical Sri Lankan dishes made with coconuts and rice were some of his favorite foods.

When he was six, Tommy moved with his parents to a small town near New York City. His parents both had new jobs there. For Tommy, life in his new town was a big surprise. Everything was different! The streets were quieter and less colorful. The grocery stores sold so many different types of fruits, vegetables, cheeses, and cereals. There were so many restaurants in his new town – he tried Italian food, Chinese food, Greek food, and Mexican food. The weather was different, too. Tommy saw snow for the very first time!

Looking back, Tommy remembers learning that the culture in the United States was different from the culture in Sri Lanka. Not better, not worse, just different. Tommy learned new things every day. He learned Spanish in school. He also learned ways that people in the U.S. communicate with each other. Tommy remembers everyone saying "How are you doing?" but it wasn't a question. It was like saying "Hi!"

Tommy was a "third culture kid." That means he was raised in a different country than his parents. Many third culture kids believe that they are lucky. They know and understand more than one culture, and they often speak more than one language. Tommy went to college in Los Angeles and studied languages. Now he works for a big charity that helps children around the world get a good education.

Sometimes it's hard to learn a whole new way of life, but Tommy says it's the best thing that ever happened. He calls Sri Lanka "home" and the U.S. "home," too!

B Read the article. Check (✓) True or False.

	True	False
1. Tommy lived in Sri Lanka most of his life.	☐	☐
2. He was born in Sri Lanka.	☐	☐
3. Tommy liked traditional Sri Lankan food.	☐	☐
4. He didn't learn any new languages in the U.S.	☐	☐
5. In the U.S., Tommy ate mostly at Sri Lankan restaurants.	☐	☐
6. Tommy is happy to be a third culture kid.	☐	☐

C Number these events in Tommy's life from 1 (first) to 8 (last).

_____ **a.** Tommy saw snow for the first time.
_____ **b.** Tommy went to college.
_____ **c.** Tommy moved to the U.S.
_____ **d.** As a small boy, Tommy played on the beach.
_____ **e.** He learned a new language in the U.S.
__1__ **f.** Tommy was born on an island.
_____ **g.** In Sri Lanka, Tommy studied English in school.
_____ **h.** He works for a charity in the U.S.

D **GROUP WORK** Tommy thinks living in another culture is a good thing. Why do you think he says that? Do you agree? Tell your classmates.

16 Can I take a message?

- Make phone calls and leave messages
- Make, accept, and decline invitations

1 CONVERSATION Please ask her to call me.

Listen and practice.

Receptionist Good morning – Creative Tours.

Nathan Hello. Can I speak to Julie Wilson, please?

Receptionist I'm sorry, but she's in a meeting right now.

Nathan Oh, OK.

Receptionist Can I take a message?

Nathan Yes, thanks. This is her friend Nathan. Please ask her to call me tonight.

Receptionist Does she have your number?

Nathan Yes, she does.

Receptionist OK. I'll give her your message.

Nathan Thank you so much.

2 WORD POWER Prepositional phrases

A Listen and practice.

at home	**at** the mall	**in** bed	**in** the shower	**on** vacation
at work	**at** the library	**in** class	**in** the hospital	**on** a trip
at school	**at** the beach	**in** Mexico	**in** a meeting	**on** his/her break

at work

on vacation

in a meeting

B **PAIR WORK** Make a list of five friends and family members. Give it to your partner. Where are these people right now? Ask and answer questions.

A: Where's your brother right now?
B: He's on vacation. He's in India.

3 LISTENING Sorry I missed your call.

A Listen to Nathan return three phone calls. Why did he miss each call? Check (✓) the correct answers.

1. He was . . .	☐ shopping.	☐ in the shower.	☐ at a party.
2. He was . . .	☐ studying.	☐ at the mall.	☐ sick.
3. He was . . .	☐ in class.	☐ sleeping.	☐ at work.

B Listen again. Why did they call Nathan? Correct the sentences.

1. Hannah called Nathan because he is having a party.
2. Andrea called Nathan because she needs to see Nathan's textbook.
3. Alexis called Nathan because Sam can come in to work on Saturday.

4 GRAMMAR FOCUS

Subject and object pronouns

Subjects		Objects	
I		**me**	
You		**you**	
He		**him**	
She got Nathan's message.	Nathan left	**her**	a message.
We		**us**	
They		**them**	

GRAMMAR PLUS *see page 147*

A Complete the phone conversations with the correct pronouns. Then practice with a partner.

1. **A:** Can ___I___ speak with Ms. Murphy, please?
   B: ________'s not here. But maybe ________ can help you.
   A: Please give ________ my new cell number. It's 555-2981.
2. **A:** Hi, this is Colin Shaw. Is Mr. Kerr there?
   B: ________'m sorry, but ________'s not here right now. Do you want to leave a message?
   A: Yes. Please tell ________ to call me at work.
3. **A:** Hello, this is Carol's Café. Are Lauren and Matt in?
   B: No, ________'re not. I'm their son. Can I help ________?
   A: ________ found their keys. ________ left ________ on the table.
   B: Just bring ________ the keys. I can give ________ to my parents.
   A: I'm sorry, but ________ can't. Can your mom or dad call ________?
   B: OK.

B **PAIR WORK** Role-play this phone conversation.

Student A: "Call" your business partner Robert White's office. You want a meeting on Monday at 4:00 P.M.

Student B: You are Robert White's assistant. Answer the phone. Mr. White is not in. Take a message.

C **PAIR WORK** Change roles. This time you want a meeting on Tuesday at 2:00 P.M.

5 SNAPSHOT

Listen and practice.

Check (✓) the activities that are popular in your country.
What other activities are popular in your country?
What are your favorite activities? Are there any activities you don't like? Why?

6 CONVERSATION Do you want to see a movie?

Listen and practice.

NATHAN Hello?

JULIE Hi, Nathan. I got your message.

NATHAN Hi. Thanks for calling me back. Sorry I called you at work.

JULIE Oh, that's OK. I was in a meeting, so I turned my cell phone off. What's up?

NATHAN Well, do you want to see a movie with me tonight?

JULIE Tonight? I'm sorry, but I can't. I have to work late tonight.

NATHAN Oh, that's too bad. How about tomorrow night?

JULIE Sure, I'd love to. What time do you want to meet?

NATHAN How about around seven o'clock at the Astoria on Pratt Avenue?

JULIE Terrific! Text me when you leave your office, OK?

7 PRONUNCIATION Reduction of *want to* and *have to*

A Listen and practice. Notice the reduction of **want to** and **have to**.

/wanə/
A: Do you **want to** go to dinner with me tonight?

/hæftə/
B: I'm sorry, but I can't. I **have to** study for a test.

B PAIR WORK Practice the conversation in Exercise 6 again. Try to reduce **want to** and **have to**.

8 GRAMMAR FOCUS

Invitations; verb + *to*

Do you want to see a play with me tonight?
Sure. **I'd** really **like to** see a good play.
I'd like to (see a play), but I **have to** work late.

I'd = I would

Would you like to go to an amusement park?
Yes, **I'd love to** (go to an amusement park)!
I'd like to (go), but I **need to** study.

GRAMMAR PLUS *see page 147*

A Complete the invitations. Then match them with the responses.

Invitations

1. Would you __like to__ go to an art festival this weekend? __d__
2. Do you ________ go to a volleyball game tomorrow night? ____
3. Would you ________ see a comedy tonight? ____
4. Do you ________ go swimming on Saturday? ____
5. Do you ________ play soccer after school today? ____
6. Would you ________ go to a hip-hop concert on Saturday night? ____

Responses

a. I'd like to, but I don't have a swimsuit!
b. I'm sorry, but I have to talk to the teacher after school.
c. I don't really like volleyball. Do you want to do something else?
d. I'd like to, but I can't. I'm going to go on a trip this weekend.
e. Yes, I'd love to. It's my favorite type of music.
f. Tonight? I can't. I need to help my parents.

B PAIR WORK Practice the invitations from part A. Respond with your own information.

A: Would you like to go to an art festival this weekend?
B: I'd like to, but I can't. I have to . . .

9 SPEAKING What is your excuse?

A Do you ever use these excuses? Check (✓) Often, Sometimes, or Never. Add your own excuse, and then compare with a partner.

	Often	Sometimes	Never
I have to work late.	☐	☐	☐
I have a headache.	☐	☐	☐
I have to babysit.	☐	☐	☐
I have a class.	☐	☐	☐
I need to do the laundry.	☐	☐	☐
I need to go to bed early.	☐	☐	☐
I need to study for a test.	☐	☐	☐
I want to visit my family.	☐	☐	☐
I'm not feeling well.	☐	☐	☐
I already have plans.	☐	☐	☐
______________________	☐	☐	☐

B Write down three things you want to do this weekend.

I want to go to the street fair on Saturday.

C **CLASS ACTIVITY** Go around the class and invite your classmates to do the things from part B. Your classmates respond with excuses.

A: Would you like to go to a concert tonight?
B: I'm sorry, but I can't. I have to work late tonight.

10 LISTENING I'll see you then!

A These four people need to change their plans. Listen to their phone calls. Who will be late? Who can't come? Check (✓) the correct answers.

	Will be late	Can't come
1. Jason	☐	☐
2. Jessica	☐	☐
3. Christian	☐	☐
4. Danielle	☐	☐

B Listen again. Who can't come? Write their first names and their excuses.

First name	**Excuse**
____________	______________________________
____________	______________________________

11 INTERCHANGE 16 The perfect weekend

Make plans with your classmates. Go to Interchange 16 on page 131.

12 READING

A Look at the guide. What type of festival is Austin City Limits?

AUSTIN CITY LIMITS!

Where to start

Some people call Austin the "Live Music Capital of the World." Every year, it hosts Austin City Limits. About 195,000 people go to this amazing festival. Most years, there are around 130 different bands that play. That's a lot of cool music to listen to!

Where's the music?

Check out the AMD stage and the Austin Ventures stage. These stages are where many musicians perform, but there are eight stages in total, so continue exploring. If you're lucky, you might hear Kendrick Lamar or Florence and the Machine! Sometimes musicians even play on a bridge.

Autograph hunters: this way!

Do you want a famous person's autograph? Look for the autograph booth. Maybe your favorite band member is there. Don't forget to take a poster or a T-shirt for the band to sign.

Snack attack

When you get hungry or thirsty, walk over to ACL Eats. It's a big food court. Local restaurants serve up delicious local food from the state of Texas. You can get salads, tacos, pizza, hot dogs, hamburgers, and drinks there. There's something for everyone.

Where to shop

Do you like to shop? Go straight to the art market – right next to the shopping center. There's a lot there – from cell phone cases to handmade African clothes. You can buy hats, photographs, books, paintings, and . . . guess what? You can even buy a guitar!

B Read the website. Check (✓) True or False.

	True	False
1. About 130,000 people go to enjoy the festival.	☐	☐
2. There are eight stages for musicians.	☐	☐
3. You can buy food at the festival, but you can't buy clothes.	☐	☐
4. ACL Eats is the name of a stage.	☐	☐
5. The art market is near the shopping center.	☐	☐
6. It's possible to get an autograph at the festival.	☐	☐

C **GROUP WORK** What events do you like to go to? Is there a special event in your city or town? Tell your classmates.

Units 15–16 Progress check

SELF-ASSESSMENT

How well can you do these things? Check (✓) the boxes.

I can . . .	Very well	OK	A little
Talk about my past (Ex. 1)	☐	☐	☐
Ask about famous people using simple past yes/no questions (Ex. 2)	☐	☐	☐
Ask and answer questions about someone's past (Ex. 2)	☐	☐	☐
Understand phone calls and leave or pass on messages (Ex. 3)	☐	☐	☐
Ask and answer questions about things I want, need, and have to do (Ex. 4)	☐	☐	☐
Make and respond to invitations (Ex. 5)	☐	☐	☐

1 SPEAKING Interview

A PAIR WORK Write three years in the first line of the chart and add your question. Ask your partner four questions about his or her life in these years and complete the chart.

	20 ____	20 ____	20 ____
How old were you in . . .?			
Who was your best friend in . . .?			
What were you like in . . .?			
__________ were / was __________ in . . .?			

B CLASS ACTIVITY Tell the class about your partner's life.

"In 2001, Leo was two. He . . ."

2 SPEAKING Who were they?

GROUP WORK Think of a famous person from the past. Your classmates ask yes/no questions to guess the person.

Was he/she born in . . . ?
Was he/she a singer? an actor? a politician?
Was he/she tall? heavy? good-looking?

A: I'm thinking of a famous man from the past.
B: Was he born in the U.S.?
A: No, he wasn't.
C: Was he . . . ?

Audrey Hepburn

Nelson Mandela

Paul Walker

3 LISTENING Give me a call!

Listen and check (✓) the best response.

1. ☐ Yes. Please tell her to call me.
   ☐ Yes. Please tell him to call me.
2. ☐ Sure. Does he have your number?
   ☐ No, sorry. He's not here right now.
3. ☐ Yes, you do.
   ☐ No, I don't.
4. ☐ I have to babysit.
   ☐ I had a terrible headache.
5. ☐ I'd love to, but I can't.
   ☐ No, I didn't go. I was at work.
6. ☐ I'm sorry. He's not here right now.
   ☐ No, Amanda is at work right now.

4 SPEAKING Find someone who . . .

A CLASS ACTIVITY Go around the class. Ask questions to complete the chart. Try to write a different name on each line.

Find someone who . . .	Name
has to babysit this weekend	
needs to do the laundry tomorrow	
wants to go home early	
wants to go shopping on Saturday	
wants to see a movie tonight	
has to go to the doctor this week	
needs to work this weekend	
doesn't want to do homework tonight	

A: Ayumi, do you have to babysit this weekend?
B: Yes, I do. I have to babysit my little sister.

B PAIR WORK Share your answers with a partner.

5 SPEAKING Would you like to . . . ?

A Make a list of five things you want to do this weekend.

B CLASS ACTIVITY Go around the class. Invite your classmates to do the things from part A. Your classmates accept or refuse the invitations.

A: Would you like to go to the Natural History Museum this weekend?
B: I'm sorry, but I can't. I have to . . .
C: Do you want to go to a soccer match on Sunday?
D: Sure, I'd love to! When would you like to . . . ?

WHAT'S NEXT?

Look at your Self-assessment again. Do you need to review anything?

This page is intentionally left blank

Interchange activities

INTERCHANGE 9 Planning a party

A You're planning a small party. Choose two sweet and two salty snacks you want to serve.

B **PAIR WORK** Get together with a partner. Compare your choices and decide on only two sweet and two salty snacks for your party.

A: Let's have pizza, popcorn, chocolates, and candy.

B: Oh, I never eat pizza and popcorn together. And I hardly ever eat chocolates or candy. Let's have pizza, hot dogs, grapes, and watermelon.

A: Well, I like grapes, but I don't like watermelon. Let's have . . .

C **GROUP WORK** Present your choices to the other pairs. Can you decide on only four snacks for the class?

INTERCHANGE 10 Hidden talents and abilities

A **CLASS ACTIVITY** Add two more activities to the list. Then go around the class. Find someone who can and someone who can't do each thing. Try to write a different name on each line.

Can you . . . ?	Can	Can't
do a handstand		
do yoga		
juggle three balls		
make your own clothes		
play two musical instruments		
raise one eyebrow		
say the alphabet backward		
say "hello" in three languages		
swim underwater		
whistle a song		

do a handstand

make your own clothes

raise one eyebrow

say the alphabet backward

whistle a song

juggle balls

A: Can you do a handstand?
B: Yes, I can. OR No, I can't.

B **CLASS ACTIVITY** Share your answers with the class.

"Nick can't do a handstand, but Sylvia can. And Yan-mei can do yoga."

C Do you have any other hidden talents or abilities?

INTERCHANGE 11 Take a guess

A **PAIR WORK** Add one more activity to the list. Is your partner going to do any of these things? Check (✓) your guesses.

	My guesses		My partner's answers	
Is your partner going to . . . ?	Yes	No	Yes	No
1. play video games tonight	☐	☐	☐	☐
2. eat special food this month	☐	☐	☐	☐
3. buy some cheese this week	☐	☐	☐	☐
4. wear a suit this month	☐	☐	☐	☐
5. wake up early tomorrow	☐	☐	☐	☐
6. have a big breakfast on Saturday	☐	☐	☐	☐
7. study for a test tomorrow night	☐	☐	☐	☐
8. drive a car over the weekend	☐	☐	☐	☐
9. get a new apartment next year	☐	☐	☐	☐
10. watch a soccer game on Sunday	☐	☐	☐	☐
11. ______________________	☐	☐	☐	☐

B **PAIR WORK** Ask and answer questions to check your guesses.

A: Are you going to play video games tonight?
B: Yes, I am. I'm going to play my favorite video game.

C **CLASS ACTIVITY** How many of your guesses are correct? Who has the most correct guesses?

INTERCHANGE 12 Problems, problems

A **PAIR WORK** Imagine you have these problems. Your partner gives advice.

I really want to buy a car, but I can't save any money. I spend every single penny I have.

I can never get up on time in the morning. I'm always late for school.

I'm new in town, and I don't know any people here. How can I make some friends?

I have a big test tomorrow. My family is very noisy, so I can't study!

My job is very stressful. I usually work 10 hours a day.

It's my best friend's birthday, and I don't have a gift for her. All the stores are closed!

A: I really want to buy a car, but . . .
B: Save some money every month. Don't . . .

B **CLASS ACTIVITY** Think of a problem you have. Then tell the class. Your classmates give advice.

A: I don't understand some vocabulary in this unit.
B: Review the unit and do your homework.
C: Don't worry. Ask the teacher.

INTERCHANGE 13A Giving directions

Student A

A PAIR WORK Look at the map. You are outside the Windsor Hotel on Oak Street between Second and Third Avenues. Ask your partner for directions to the three places below. Your map does not have names on these buildings, but your partner's map does. Listen to your partner, find the places on the map, and write their names.

garage	supermarket	flower shop

A: Excuse me. How do I get to the garage?
B: Walk down Maple Street to First Avenue. Turn . . .

B PAIR WORK Your partner asks you for directions to three places. Your partner's map does not have names on these buildings, but your map does. Use the expressions in the box to give directions.

Go up/Go down . . .	It's on the corner of . . . Street	It's next to . . .
Walk up/Walk down . . .	and . . . Avenue.	It's behind . . .
Turn right/Turn left . . .	It's between . . . and . . .	It's in front of . . .
It's across from . . .		

INTERCHANGE 13B Giving directions

Student B

A **PAIR WORK** Look at the map. You are outside the Windsor Hotel on Oak Street between Second and Third Avenues. Your partner asks you for directions to three places. Your partner's map does not have names on these buildings, but your map does. Use the expressions in the box to give directions.

A: Excuse me. How do I get to the garage?

B: Walk down Oak Street to First Avenue. Turn . . .

Go up/Go down . . .	It's on the corner of . . . Street	It's next to . . .
Walk up/Walk down . . .	and . . . Avenue.	It's behind . . .
Turn right/Turn left . . .	It's between . . . and . . .	It's in front of . . .
It's across from . . .		

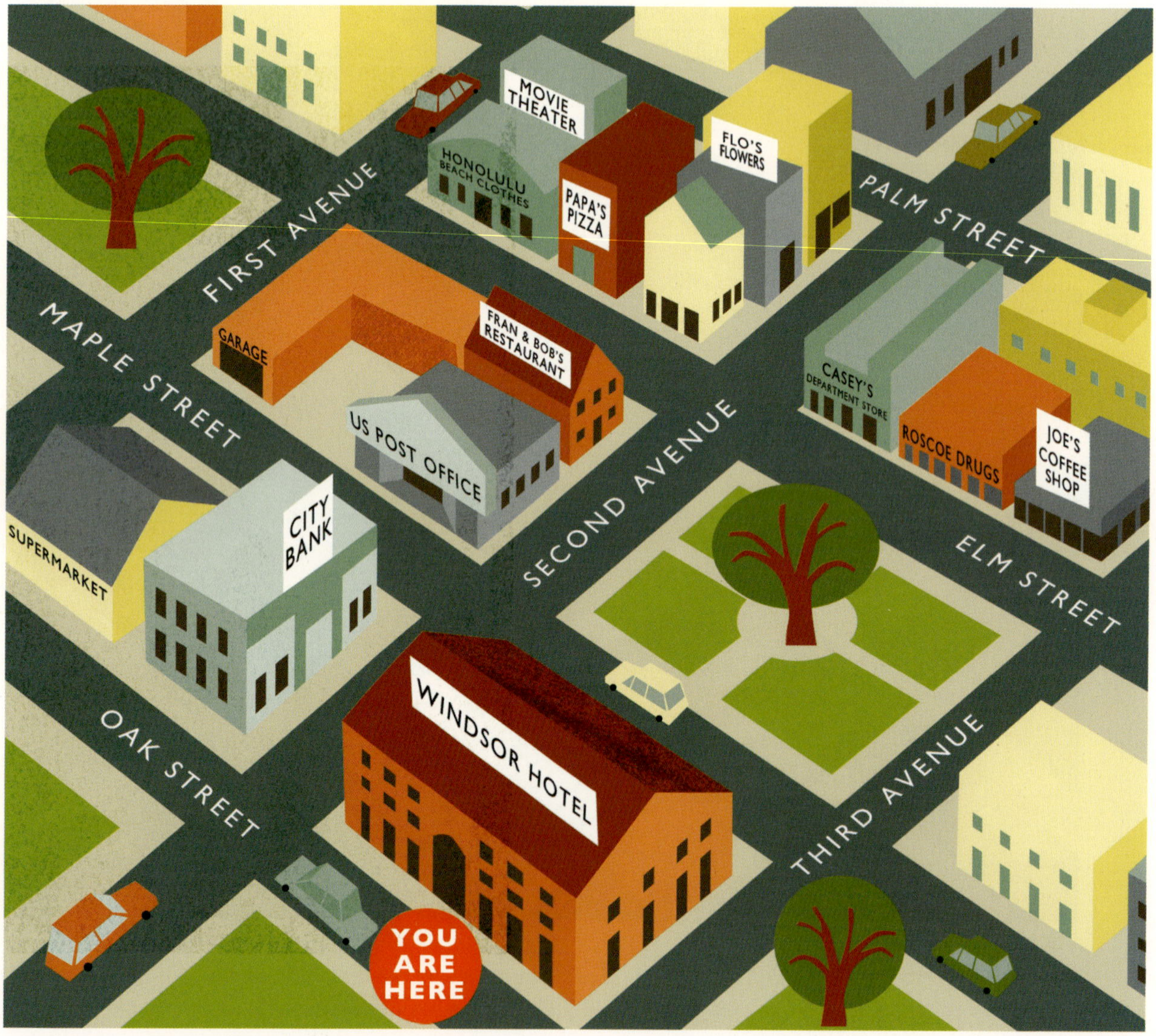

B **PAIR WORK** Ask your partner for directions to the three places below. Your map does not have names on these buildings, but your partner's map does. Listen to your partner, find the places on the map and write their names.

coffee shop	shoe store	bookstore

INTERCHANGE 14 Past activities

A PAIR WORK What did you do when you were a child? First, check (✓) your answers to the questions. Then ask your partner the same questions. Check (✓) your partner's answers.

A: Did you argue with your friends as a child?
B: Yes, I did. OR No, I didn't.

A: Did you clean your room?
B: Yes, I did. OR No, I didn't.

argue with your friends

	Me		My partner	
Did you . . . as a child?	**Yes**	**No**	**Yes**	**No**
argue with your friends	☐	☐	☐	☐
clean your room	☐	☐	☐	☐
make your bed	☐	☐	☐	☐
get up early on weekdays	☐	☐	☐	☐
sleep late on weekends	☐	☐	☐	☐
have a tablet	☐	☐	☐	☐
play video games	☐	☐	☐	☐
listen to rock music	☐	☐	☐	☐
play a musical instrument	☐	☐	☐	☐
play a sport	☐	☐	☐	☐
ride a bicycle	☐	☐	☐	☐
wear braces	☐	☐	☐	☐

wear braces

make your bed

play a musical instrument

B PAIR WORK Join another pair. Tell them what your partner did and didn't do as a child.

"Yu-jin didn't argue with her friends as a child. She cleaned her room."

INTERCHANGE 15 This is your life

A What were five important events in your life? Choose four events and add another important event. Then write the years when these events happened in the box.

I was born in . . .

I started elementary school in . . .

I went to my first musical concert in . . .

I opened my first bank account in . . .

I traveled with friends in . . .

I graduated from high school in . . .

I moved to a new place in . . .

I started learning English in . . .

I . . . in . . .

Years

1. ____________
2. ____________
3. ____________
4. ____________
5. ____________

B **PAIR WORK** Ask your partner about his or her life events. Your partner will only show you the box with the years.

A: What happened in 2002?
B: I started elementary school.

A: How old were you?
B: I was six.

INTERCHANGE 16 The perfect weekend

A You are planning your dream weekend. Write your plans for Saturday and Sunday in the charts. Use these expressions and your own ideas.

go to (the movies/a party)	play (basketball/video games)
go (dancing/shopping)	meet (my friend/teacher)
go (on a trip/picnic)	have dinner with (my brother/parents)
study for (a test/an exam)	visit (my parents/grandparents)
go out with (my girlfriend/boyfriend)	see (the dentist/doctor)

WEEKEND PLANS

Saturday	Me	My partner
morning	____________	____________
lunch	____________	____________
afternoon	____________	____________
evening	____________	____________
dinner	____________	____________
after dinner	____________	____________

WEEKEND PLANS

Sunday	Me	My partner
morning	____________	____________
lunch	____________	____________
afternoon	____________	____________
evening	____________	____________
dinner	____________	____________
after dinner	____________	____________

B **PAIR WORK** Compare your plans with your partner. Choose activities to do together.

A: What do you want to do on Saturday morning?
B: Let's go swimming. They opened a new pool at the gym.
A: Oh, I can't swim. Sorry. Maybe we can go bike riding . . .

C **GROUP WORK** Join another pair. Can you decide what to do over the weekend together?

A: So, would you like to go bike riding on Saturday morning?
C: Good idea. And how about a barbecue for lunch?
B: Oh, we don't have time for a barbecue. We want to go to an art festival in the afternoon . . .

Grammar plus

UNIT 9

1 Count and noncount nouns; *some* and *any* page 59

- Count nouns name things you can count: *bananas, crackers, carrots*. Count nouns have a singular and plural form: ***1 orange, 2 oranges***. Noncount nouns name things you can't count: *milk, oil, rice*.
- Use *some* in affirmative sentences: We have **some** butter. Use *any* in negative sentences and questions: We don't have **any** lettuce. Do we have **any** tomatoes?

Complete the conversations with *some* or *any*.

1. **A:** What do you want for lunch?
   B: Let's make ___some___ sandwiches.
   A: Good idea! We have ______________ bread. Do we have ______________ cheese?
   B: Yes, I think there's ______________ in the refrigerator. Let me see. . . .
   No, I don't see ______________.
   A: Well, let's go to the store. We need ______________ milk, too.
   And do we have ______________ cheese?
   B: Yes, we do. There's ______________ lettuce here, and there are ______________ tomatoes, too.
   A: Do we have ______________ mayonnaise? I love ______________ mayonnaise on my sandwiches.
   B: Me, too. But there isn't ______________ here. Let's buy ______________.
2. **A:** Let's make a big breakfast tomorrow morning.
   B: Good idea! What do we need? Are there ______________ eggs?
   A: There are ______________ but I think we need to buy ______________ more.
   B: OK. And let's get ______________ cereal, too. We don't have ______________, and I love cereal for breakfast.
   A: Me, too. Do we have ______________ blueberry yogurt?
   B: Yes, there's ______________ in the refrigerator.
   A: Great! So we don't need to buy ______________ at the store.
   B: That's right. Just eggs and cereal!

2 Adverbs of frequency page 61

- Adverbs of frequency usually go before the main verb: *always, almost always, usually, often, sometimes, hardly ever, almost never, never*: She **never eats** breakfast. I **almost always have** tea in the morning. *Sometimes* can also begin a sentence: **Sometimes** I **eat** broccoli.

Rewrite the conversation. Add the adverbs in the correct places.

A: Where do you have lunch? (usually)	*Where do you usually have lunch?*
B: I go to a restaurant near work. (often)	______________
A: Do you eat at your desk? (ever)	______________
B: No, I stay in for lunch. (hardly ever)	______________
A: And what do you have? (usually)	______________
B: I have soup or a salad. (always)	______________
A: Me, too. I have a big lunch. (never)	______________

UNIT 10

1 Simple present Wh-questions page 65

- Remember: *Who* = what person; *where* = what place; *how often* = what frequency; *when* = what days; *what time* = what time of day
- Remember: Use *do* or *does* after the question word.

Complete the questions with the correct question word and *do* or *does*. Then match the questions with the answers.

1. What sport do you like? c
2. ________ you go to games with? ____
3. ________ often ________ your team play? ____
4. ________ they play? ____
5. ________ they play? ____
6. ________ time ________ the games start? ____

a. My father and my two brothers.
b. Usually at four o'clock.
c. Soccer. I love to watch my team.
d. Once or twice a month.
e. On Sunday afternoons.
f. At the Olympic Stadium.

2 *Can* for ability page 67

- Use the base form of the verb with *can*. With third-person singular, don't add an *–s* to *can* or to the base form: She **can play** the piano. (NOT: ~~She can plays the piano.~~)

A Write sentences about the things people can and can't do. Use *can* or *can't* with *and*, *but*, or *or*. (✓ = can, ✗ = can't)

1. Olivia: ride a bike ✓ drive a car ✗
   Olivia can ride a bike, but she can't drive a car.
2. Juan: play the piano ✓ play the violin ✓
   ____
3. Matt and Drew: act ✓ sing ✗
   ____
4. Alicia: snowboard ✓ ice-skate ✗
   ____
5. Ben: take good photos ✓ edit videos ✓
   ____
6. Corinne: write poems ✗ tell good jokes ✓
   ____

B Look at part A. Answer the questions. Write short sentences.

1. Can Matt and Drew sing? No, they can't.
2. Who can tell good jokes? ________________
3. Can Olivia drive a car? ________________
4. Can Juan play the piano? ________________
5. Who can snowboard? ________________
6. What can Matt do? ________________

UNIT 11

1 The future with *be going to* page 73

- Use *am/is/are* + *going to* + base form for the future: We**'re going to have** dinner with my parents tonight.
- In questions with *be going to*, the *be* verb comes before the subject: **Is he going to buy** me a gift?

A Complete Matthew's story. Use the correct form of *be going to* and the verbs in parentheses.

Tomorrow is ___going to be___ (be) a very exciting day. It's my birthday, and my friends and I ____________ (celebrate). In the morning, Stephen and I ____________ (drive) to the beach. Our friend Rosa ____________ (meet) us there. We ____________ (stay) at the beach for a few hours. Then we ____________ (have) lunch at my favorite restaurant. After lunch, Stephen ____________ (go) to work, and Rosa and I ____________ (see) a movie. After the movie, we ____________ (go) to our friend Philip's house. He ____________ (make) his special homemade pizza for Rosa and me.

B Write questions. Then look at part A and answer the questions.

1. Matthew / celebrate / with his family?
   Q: _Is Matthew going to celebrate with his family?_
   A: _No, he's going to celebrate with his friends._
2. Stephen and Matthew / ride their bikes / to the beach?
   Q: ____________
   A: ____________
3. the friends / have lunch / at a restaurant?
   Q: ____________
   A: ____________
4. Rosa and Matthew / go to a museum?
   Q: ____________
   A: ____________
5. Rosa and Matthew / have pizza / at a restaurant?
   Q: ____________
   A: ____________

2 Wh-questions with *be going to* page 75

- Use *is* in questions with *Who* as the subject: **Who's** going to be there? (NOT: ~~Who are going to be there?~~)

Complete the conversation with the correct form of *be going to*.

A: What ___are___ you ___going to do___ (do) this weekend?
B: I ____________ (have) a very busy weekend. My friend Amir ____________ (visit) me, and we ____________ (spend) the weekend in the city.
A: That's nice. ________ you ____________ (stay) in a hotel?
B: No, we ____________ (stay) with our friend Lara. And Lara ____________ (have) a big party on Saturday night.
A: Really? And who ____________ (be) at the party? Do you know any of Lara's friends?
B: No, I don't. But Amir and I ____________ (meet) everyone on Saturday night.

UNIT 12

1 *Have* + noun; *feel* + adjective page 79

- For most health problems, use *a/an*: I have **a** cold. I have **an** earache. With *flu*, use *the*: I have **the** flu. (NOT: ~~I have a flu.~~)

Complete the conversation. Use the sentences in the box.

> **I think I have a fever.**
> **Thanks.**
> **I feel awful, actually.**
> **Yes. I'm going to call my doctor in a few minutes.**
> **Yes, I do. And I have a stomachache, too.**
> ✓ **Hi, Vanessa. How are you?**

A: *Hi, Vanessa. How are you?*
B: I'm terrific, thanks. How about you?
A: ________________
B: Oh, no! What's the matter?
A: ________________
B: That's too bad. Do you have a headache?
A: ________________
B: Are you going to see a doctor?
A: ________________
B: Well, feel better soon.
A: ________________

2 Imperatives page 82

- Use the base form of the verb in affirmative imperatives: **Go** home and **rest**, Ms. Lake.
- Use *don't* + base form of the verb in negative imperatives. The form doesn't change: **Don't go** to work today, Ms. Lake.

Read the situations. Give the people advice. Use the phrases in the box.

> ✓ **drink coffee in the evening**
> **eat any cold food**
> **exercise today or tomorrow**
> **take an antacid**
> **take two aspirins**
> **work too hard**

1. Dave: "I can't sleep at night." *Don't drink coffee in the evening.*
2. Corey: "I have a headache." ________________
3. Lucia: "I work 12 hours a day." ________________
4. William: "My legs hurt." ________________
5. Min-ho: "I have a toothache." ________________
6. Fatima: "I have an awful stomachache." ________________

UNIT 13

1 Prepositions of place page 88

- Use *on* with the names of streets and avenues: The bookstore is **on** Center Street. The theater is **on** Park Avenue.
- *Across from* is another way of saying *opposite*: The library is **across from** the theater. = The library is **opposite** the theater.

Choose the correct words.

A: Excuse me. Is there a post office around here?
B: Yes, there is. It's **in / (on)** Maple Street.
A: Where on Maple?
B: It's **in / on** the corner of Maple Street and Second Avenue.
A: Next **from / to** Charlie's Restaurant?
B: Yes, that's right. It's across the street **from** / **to** the Windsor Hotel.
A: Thanks. Oh, and where is the bank?
B: It's on Oak Street – **between / next to** the hospital and police station.
A: Great. Thanks very much.
B: You're welcome.

2 Directions page 90

- *Walk up/Go up* mean the same thing. *Walk down/Go down* also mean the same thing.

Jenna doesn't know Manhattan at all. Correct Jenna's directions.
Write the opposite of what she says.

1. Cal: How do I get to Washington Square Park?
Jenna: Walk up Fifth Avenue.
You: *No, don't walk up Fifth Avenue. Walk down Fifth Avenue.*

2. Cal: How can I get to the Empire State Building?
Jenna: Turn right on 32nd Street.
You: ______________________________

3. Cal: How do I get to Bryant Park from Rockefeller Center?
Jenna: Go down Sixth Avenue.
You: ______________________________
Jenna: It's on the left.
You: ______________________________

4. Cal: How do I get to Central Park?
Jenna: Walk down Eighth Avenue.
You: ______________________________

UNIT 14

1 Simple past statements: regular verbs and irregular verbs

page 93–94

- Use simple past verbs to talk about the past. Regular verbs end in *–ed*: I **watched** TV last night. For verbs ending in *–e*, add *–d*: *live* ⟶ *lived*. For verbs ending in vowel + consonant, double the consonant and add *–ed*: *shop* ⟶ *shopped*.
- Use *didn't* + base form in negative statements. The form doesn't change: He **didn't shop** for groceries yesterday. (NOT: ~~He didn't shopped for groceries yesterday.~~)

Maya wrote an email to a friend. Complete the sentences with the simple past form of the verbs in parentheses.

Hi!

I ___didn't do___ (not do) anything special this weekend, but I ___________ (have) a lot of fun. I ___________ (not go) out on Friday night. I ___________ (stay) home. I ___________ (clean) my room and ___________ (do) the laundry. I ___________ (help) my sister with her homework, and then we ___________ (watch) our favorite series. On Saturday, my friend Lori ___________ (come) over. She ___________ (need) some new shoes, so we ___________ (take) the bus downtown to Todd's Shoe Store. We ___________ (shop) for a long time, but Lori ___________ (not like) any of the shoes at Todd's. She ___________ (buy) some purple socks, but she ___________ (not buy) any shoes. On our way back to my house, we ___________ (stop) at the gym and ___________ (exercise). We ___________ (not exercise) very hard. I ___________ (invite) Lori for dinner, and my dad ___________ (cook) hamburgers in the yard. After dinner, Lori and I ___________ (talk) and ___________ (play) video games. She ___________ (not stay) very late – my mother ___________ (drive) her home at around ten. On Sunday, my whole family ___________ (visit) my mother's best friend and her family. They have a swimming pool, so my sister and I ___________ (go) swimming all afternoon.

Tell me about your weekend!

Maya

2 Simple past yes/no questions

page 95

- Use *did* + base form in questions. The form doesn't change: **Did** you **have** fun yesterday? (NOT: ~~Did you had fun yesterday?~~)

Complete the conversation. Use the simple past form of the verbs in parentheses.

A: ___Did___ you ___enjoy___ (enjoy) your vacation?
B: Yes, I ___________. My brother and I ___________ (have) a great time.
A: ___________ you ___________ (make) any videos?
B: No, we ___________. But we ___________ (take) a lot of pictures.
A: That's good. ___________ you ___________ (see) a lot of interesting things?
B: Yes, we ___________. And we ___________ (eat) a lot of new foods. How about you? ___________ you (have) a good summer?
A: Well, I ___________ (not go) anywhere, but I ___________ (read) a lot of good books and ___________ (see) some great movies.

UNIT 15

1 Past of *be* page 101

■ Present		Past
am/is	→	**was**
are	→	**were**

Complete the conversations with *was, wasn't, were,* or *weren't.*

1. **A:** ___Were___ you here yesterday?
   B: No, I ____________. I ____________ home in bed.
   A: Oh, ____________ you sick?
   B: No. I ____________ just really tired.
2. **A:** Where ____________ you born?
   B: I ____________ born in Mexico City.
   A: Really? What about your parents? ____________ they born here, too?
   B: No, they ____________.They ____________ born in Guadalajara.
3. **A:** Where ____________ Jamil last week? ____________ he on vacation?
   B: Yes, he ____________. He and his best friend ____________ in Portugal. They ____________ in Oporto.
   A: ____________ it a good trip?
   B: Yes, it was. Jamil said it ____________ a terrific trip!

2 Wh-questions with *did, was,* and *were* page 101

- Don't use *did* with the past of *be*: Where **were** you last Tuesday? (NOT: ~~Where did you were last Tuesday?~~) Use *did* in simple past questions with other verbs: Where **did** you **go** last Tuesday?
- *Because* answers the question *Why?*

Complete the questions. Use the words in the box.

✓ **how**	**what**	**where**	**why**
how old	**when**	**who**	

1. **A:** ___How___ was your childhood?
   B: I had a fantastic childhood!
2. **A:** ____________ did you grow up?
   B: I grew up in Incheon, a small city in South Korea.
3. **A:** ____________ were you when you started school?
   B: I think I was five or six.
4. **A:** ____________ was your best friend in high school?
   B: My best friend was a boy named Joon-ho.
5. **A:** ____________ did you leave home?
   B: In 2012.
6. **A:** ____________ did you leave Incheon?
   B: Because I wanted to live in a big city.
7: **A:** ____________ was your first job in Seoul?
   B: I worked as a server in a restaurant.

UNIT 16

1 Subject and object pronouns page 107

- Subject pronouns usually come before verbs, and object pronouns go after verbs: **I** saw **him**, but **he** didn't see **me**.

Complete the conversations.

1. **A:** Hello. Is Mr. Chang there?
   B: No, ___he___ 's not here right now. Can I take a message?
   A: Yes. Please tell ______ to call Todd Harris.
   B: Does ______ have your number?
   A: No, but please give it to ______. It's 555-0987.
2. **A:** Oh, hello, Kimberly!
   A: Hello, Mrs. Sanchez. Is Veronica home?
   B: No, ______ at the mall with her brother. Their dad drove ______ there this morning. Would ______ like to come in?
   A: Thank you, Mrs. Sanchez, but I need to go home. Anyway, my sister and ______ are going to an amusement park tomorrow and maybe Veronica can go with ______. Is that all right?
   B: Sure. I can give ______ your message, or ______ can text her.
   A: Oh, don't worry, Mrs. Sanchez. I'll text ______. Thanks a lot. Bye!

2 Invitations; verb + *to* page 109

- You can use both *Do you want to . . . ?* and *Would you like to . . . ?* to invite a person to do something.
- Don't confuse *would like to* with *like to*. *Would like to* means the same as *want to*.
- *I'd (really) like to* and *I'd love to* both mean the same as *I want to*.

Rewrite the conversations. Write the sentences in a different way.

1.	**A:** Do you want to see a movie tonight?	**A:**	Would you like to see a movie tonight?
	B: Oh, I can't. I need to work.	**B:**	
2.	**A:** Do you want to play tennis on Saturday?	**A:**	
	B: I'd love to, but I have to help my parents.	**B:**	
3.	**A:** I want a job at Carol's café.	**A:**	
	B: You need to speak to her.	**B:**	
4.	**A:** Would you like to go to a party with me?	**A:**	
	B: I want to, but I can't. I have to study.	**B:**	

Grammar plus answer key

Unit 9

1 Count and noncount nouns; *some* and *any*

1. A: What do you want for lunch?
 B: Let's make **some** sandwiches.
 A: Good idea! We have **some** bread. Do we have **any** cheese?
 B: Yes, I think there's **some** in the refrigerator. Let me see. . . . No, I don't see **any**.
 A: Well, let's go to the store. We need **some** milk, too. And do we have **any** cheese?
 B: Yes, we do. There's **some** lettuce here, and there are **some** tomatoes, too.
 A: Do we have **any** mayonnaise? I love **some** mayonnaise on my sandwiches.
 B: Me, too. But there isn't **any** here. Let's buy **some**.
2. A: Let's make a big breakfast tomorrow morning.
 B: Good idea! What do we need? Are there **any** eggs?
 A: There are **some** but I think we need to buy **some** more.
 B: OK. And let's get **some** cereal, too. We don't have **any**, and I love cereal for breakfast.
 A: Me, too. Do we have **any** blueberry yogurt?
 B: Yes, there's **some** in the refrigerator.
 A: Great! So we don't need to buy **any** at the store.
 B: That's right. Just eggs and cereal!

2 Adverbs of frequency (page 61)

B: I often go to a restaurant near work.
A: Do you ever eat at your desk?
B: No, I hardly ever stay in for lunch.
A: A: And what do you usually have?
B: I always have soup or a salad.
A: Me, too. I never have a big lunch.

Unit 10

1 Simple present Wh-questions

2. Who do you go to games with? a
3. How often does your team play? d
4. When do they play? e or Where do they play? f
5. Where do they play? f or When do they play? e
6. What time do the games start? b

2 *Can* for ability

A

2. Juan can play the piano, and he can play the violin.
3. Matt and Drew can act, but they can't sing.
4. Alicia can snowboard, but she can't ice-skate.
5. Ben can take good photos, and he can edit videos.
6. Corinne can't write poems but she can tell good jokes.

B

2. Corinne can.
4. Yes, he can.
6. He can act.
3. No, she can't.
5. Alicia can.

Unit 11

1 The future with *be going to*

A Tomorrow **is going to be** a very exciting day. It's my birthday, and my friends and I **are going to celebrate**. In the morning, Stephen and I **are going to drive** to the beach. Our friend Rosa **is going to meet** us there. We**'re going to stay** at the beach for a few hours. Then we**'re going to have** lunch at my favorite restaurant. After lunch, Stephen **is going to go** to work, and Rosa and I **are going to see** a movie. After the movie, we**'re going to go** to our friend Philip's house. He **is going to cook** dinner for Rosa and me.

B Q: Are Stephen and Matthew going to ride their bikes to the beach?
 A: No, they're going to drive to the beach.
4. Q: Are the friends going to have lunch at a restaurant?
 A: Yes, they are.
5. Q: Are Rosa and Matthew going to go to a museum?
 A: No, they're not. (They're going to see a movie.)
6. Q: Are Rosa and Matthew going to have dinner at a restaurant?
 A: No, they're not. (They're going to have dinner at Philip's house.)

2 Wh-questions with *be going to*

A: What **are** you **going to do** this weekend?
B: I**'m going to have** a very busy weekend. My friend Amir **is going to visit** me, and we**'re going to spend** the weekend in the city.
A: That's nice. **Are** you **going to stay** in a hotel?
B: No, we**'re going to stay** with our friend Lara. And Lara **is going to have** a big party on Saturday night.
A: Really? And who**'s going to be** at the party? Do you know any of Lara's friends?
B: No, I don't. But Amir and I **are going to meet** everyone on Saturday night.

Unit 12

1 *Have* + noun; *feel* + adjective

A: **Hi, Vanessa. How are you?**
B: I'm terrific, thanks. How about you?
A: **I feel awful, actually.**
B: Oh, no! What's the matter?
A: **I think I have a fever.**
B: That's too bad. Do you have a headache?
A: **Yes, I do. And I have a stomachache, too.**
B: Are you going to see a doctor?
A: **Yes. I'm going to call my doctor in a few minutes.**
B: Well, feel better soon.
A: **Thanks.**

2 Imperatives

2. Take two aspirins.
3. Don't work too hard.
4. Don't exercise today or tomorrow.
5. Don't eat any cold food.
6. Take an antacid.

Unit 13

1 Prepositions of place

A: Excuse me. Is there a post office around here?
B: Yes, there is. It's **on** Maple Street.
A: Where on Maple?
B: It's **on** the corner of Maple Street and Second Avenue.
A: Next **to** Charlie's Restaurant?
B: Yes, that's right. It's across the street **from** the Windsor Hotel.
A: Thanks. Oh, and where is the bank?
B: It's on Oak Street – **between** the hospital and police station.
A: Great. Thanks very much.
B: You're welcome.

2 Directions

2. You: No, don't turn right on 32nd Street. Turn left on 32nd Street.
3. You: No, don't go down Sixth Avenue. Go up First Avenue.
   You: No, it's not on the left. It's on the right.
4. You: No, don't walk down Eight Avenue. Walk up Eighth Avenue.

Unit 14

1 Simple past statements: regular verbs and irregular verbs

Hi!
I **didn't do** anything special this weekend, but I **had** a lot of fun. I **didn't go** out on Friday night. I **stayed** home. I **cleaned** my room and **did** laundry. I **helped** my sister with her homework, and then we **watched** our favorite series. On Saturday, my friend Lori **came** over. She **needed** some new shoes, so we **took** the bus downtown to Todd's Shoe Store. We **shopped** for a long time, but Lori **didn't like** any of the shoes at Todd's. She **bought** some purple socks, but she **didn't buy** any shoes. On our way back to my house, we **stopped** at the gym and **exercised**. We **didn't exercise** very hard. I **invited** Lori for dinner, and my dad **cooked** hamburgers in the yard. After dinner, Lori and I **talked** and **played** video games. She **didn't stay** too late – Mom **drove** her home at around ten. On Sunday, my whole family **visited** my mother's best friend and her family. They have a swimming pool, so my sister and I **went** swimming all afternoon.

2 Simple past yes/no questions

A: **Did** you **enjoy** your vacation?
B: Yes, I **did**. My brother and I **had** a great time.
A: **Did** you **make** a lot any videos?
B: No, we **didn't**. But we **took** a lot of pictures.
A: That's good. **Did** you **see** a lot of interesting things?
B: Yes, we **did**. And we **ate** a lot of new foods. How about you? **Did** you **have** a good summer?
A: Well, I **didn't go** anywhere, but I **read** a lot of good books and **saw** some great movies.

Unit 15

1 Past of *be*

1. A: **Were** you here yesterday?
   B: No, I **wasn't**. I **was** home in bed.
   A: Oh, **were** you sick?
   B: No. I **was** just really tired.
2. A: Where **were** you born?
   B: I **was** born in Mexico City.
   A: Really? What about your parents? **Were** they born here, too?
   B: No, they **weren't**. They **were** born in Guadalajara.
3. A: Where **was** Jamil last week? **Was** he on vacation?
   B: Yes, he **was**. He and his best friend **were** in Portugal. They **were** in Oporto.
   A: **Was** it a good trip?
   B: Yes, it was. Jamil said it **was** a terrific trip!

2 Wh-questions with *did, was,* and *were*

1. A: **How** was your childhood?
   B: I had a fantastic childhood!
2. A: **Where** did you grow up?
   B: I grew up in Incheon, a small city in South Korea.
3. A: **How old** were you when you started school?
   B: I think I was five or six.
4. A: **Who** was your best friend in high school?
   B: My best friend was a boy named Joon-ho.
5. A: **When** did you leave home?
   B: In 2012.
6. A: **Why** did you leave Incheon?
   B: Because I wanted to live in a big city.
7: A: **What** was your first job in Seoul?
   B: I worked as a server in a restaurant.

Unit 16

1 Subject and object pronouns

1. A: Hello. Is Mr. Chang there?
   B: No, **he's** not here right now. Can take a message?
   A: Yes. Please tell **him** to call Todd Harris.
   B: Does **he** have your number?
   A: No, but please give it to **him**. It's 555-0987.
2. A: Oh, hello, Kimberly!
   A: Hello, Mrs. Sanchez. Is Veronica home?
   B: No, **she's** at the mall with her brother. Their dad drove **them** there this morning. Would **you** like to come in?
   A: Thank you, Mrs. Sanchez, but I need to go home. Anyway, my sister and **I** are going to an amusement park tomorrow and maybe Veronica can go with **us**. Is that all right?
   B: Sure. I can give **her** your message, or **you** can text her.
   A: Oh, don't worry, Mrs. Sanchez. I'll text **her.** Thanks a lot. Bye!

2 Invitations; verb + *to*

1. B: Oh, I can't. I **have** to work.
2. A: **Would you like** to play tennis on Saturday?
   B: **I'd like to,** but I need to help my parents.
3. A: **I'd like** a job at Carol's café.
   B: You **have** to speak to her.
4. A: **Do you want** to go to a party with me?
   B: **I'd like to**, but I can't. I **need** to study.

Credits

The authors and publishers acknowledge the following sources of copyright material and are grateful for the permissions granted. While every effort has been made, it has not always been possible to identify the sources of all the material used, or to trace all copyright holders. If any omissions are brought to our notice, we will be happy to include the appropriate acknowledgements on reprinting and in the next update to the digital edition, as applicable.

Key: B = Below, BL = Below Left, BC = Below Centre, BR = Below Right, B/G = Background, C = Centre, CL = Centre Left, CR = Centre Right, Ex = Exercise, TC = Top Centre, T = Top, TL = Top Left, TR = Top Right.

Illustrations

337 Jon (KJA Artists): 24, 29, 85; **Mark Duffin**: 15, 12(T), 31(T), 44(T), 47, 115, 121; **Thomas Girard** (Good Illustration): 3, 11, 13, 23, 25, 36, 37, 50, 79(T), 89, 100, 102; **Dusan Lakicevic** (Beehive Illustration): 21, 41, 87; **Quino Marin** (The Organisation): 26, 31(B), 79(B); **Gavin Reece** (New Division): 27, 44(B), 45, 101; **Gary Venn** (Lemonade Illustration): 56, 88, 90, 91, 127, 128; **Paul Williams** (Sylvie Poggio Artists): 9, 30, 119.

Photos

Back cover (woman with whiteboard): Jenny Acheson/Stockbyte/GettyImages; Back cover (whiteboard): Nemida/GettyImages; Back cover (man using phone): Betsie Van Der Meer/Taxi/GettyImages; Back cover (woman smiling): PeopleImages.com/DigitalVision/GettyImages; Back cover (name tag): Tetra Images/GettyImages; Back cover (handshake): David Lees/Taxi/GettyImages; p. v: PhotoAlto/Sigrid Olsson/PhotoAlto Agency RF Collections/GettyImages; p. 58 (header), p. viii (unit 9): Johner Images/GettyImages; p. 58 (apples): Maximilian Stock Ltd/Photolibrary/GettyImages; p. 58 (lemons): osoznaniejizni/iStock/GettyImages; p. 58 (bananas): Burazin/Photographer's Choice/GettyImages; p. 58 (kiwis): serebryakova/iStock/GettyImages; p. 58 (blueberries): Richard Coombs/EyeEm/EyeEm/GettyImages; p. 58 (oranges): David Marsden/Photolibrary/GettyImages; p. 58 (tomatoes): James A. Guilliam/Photolibrary/GettyImages; p. 58 (onions): Joff Lee/StockFood Creative/GettyImages; p. 58 (lettuce): Richard Clark/Photolibrary/GettyImages; p. 58 (carrots): Maximilian Stock Ltd./Photolibrary/GettyImages; p. 58 (potatoes): SvetlanaK/iStock/GettyImages; p. 58 (broccoli): Tsuji/E+/GettyImages; p. 58 (pasta): Dave King Dorling Kindersley/Dorling Kindersley/GettyImages; p. 58 (noodles): Yoyochow23/iStock/GettyImages; p. 58 (rice): Maximilian Stock Ltd/Photolibrary/GettyImages; p. 58 (crackers): Richard Griffin/iStock/GettyImages; p. 58 (bread): Pavlo_K/iStock/GettyImages; p. 58 (cereal): Graham Day/Photolibrary/GettyImages; p. 58 (butter): DustyPixel/E+/GettyImages; p. 58 (mayonnaise): Suzifoo/E+/GettyImages; p. 58 (oil): John E. Kelly/Photolibrary/GettyImages; p. 58 (cheese): jjwithers/E+/GettyImages; p. 58 (milk): PhotoObjects.net/PhotoObjects.net/GettyImages; p. 58 (cream): malerapaso/E+/GettyImages; p. 58 (yogurt): Science Photo Library/Science Photo Library/GettyImages; p. 58 (beans): malerapaso/iStock/GettyImages; p. 58 (nuts): Maximilian Stock Ltd./Photographer's Choice/GettyImages; p. 58 (eggs): ermingut/E+/GettyImages; p. 58 (beef): Lew Robertson/StockFood Creative/GettyImages; p. 58 (chicken): Andrea Bricco/StockFood Creative/GettyImages; p. 58 (fish): angorius/iStock/GettyImages; p. 59 (TR): RyanJLane/E+/GettyImages; p. 59 (potato salad): JFsPic/iStock/GettyImages; p. 59 (potato): -massmedia-/iStock/Getty Images Plus/GettyImages; p. 59 (celery): anna1311/iStock/GettyImages; p. 59 (onions): prwstd/iStock/GettyImages; p. 59 (mayonnaise): BWFolsom/iStock/GettyImages; p. 59 (apple): Raimondas/iStock/GettyImages; p. 60 (oranges): JannHuizenga/iStock/Getty Images Plus/GettyImages; p. 60 (apples): joanek/iStock/GettyImages; p. 60 (lettuce): Foodcollection RF/GettyImages; p. 60 (potatoes): RBOZUK/iStock/GettyImages; p. 60 (tomatoes): S847/iStock/Getty Images Plus/GettyImages; p. 60 (celery): Stefano Oppo/Stockbyte/GettyImages; p. 60 (bananas): PavlinaGab/iStock/Getty Images Plus/GettyImages; p. 60 (kiwis): nullplus/iStock/Getty Images Plus/GettyImages; p. 60 (lemons): Michael Paul/StockFood Creative/GettyImages; p. 60 (carrots): RBOZUK/iStock/GettyImages; p. 60 (onions): IJdema/iStock/GettyImages; p. 60 (broccoli): Marco Vacca/Photographer's Choice RF/GettyImages; p. 60 (blueberries): billnoll/iStock/Getty Images Plus/GettyImages; p. 60 (BL): Rohit Seth/iStock/GettyImages; p. 60 (BC): MIXA/GettyImages; p. 60 (BR): Alberto Coto/Photodisc/GettyImages; p. 61 (TR): artparadigm/Taxi Japan/GettyImages; p. 61 (BR): Luis Alvarez/Taxi/GettyImages; p. 62: LiudmylaSupynska/iStock/Getty Images Plus/GettyImages; p. 63 (CR): Mardis Coers/Moment/GettyImages; p. 63 (TL): BIEL ALINO/AFP/GettyImages; p. 63 (CL): gnomeandi/iStock/GettyImages; p. 63 (BR): Danita Delimont/Gallo Images/GettyImages; p. 64 (header), p. viii (unit 10): Mike Powell/Allsport Concepts/GettyImages; p. 64 (racket): Arijuhani/iStock/Getty Images Plus/GettyImages; p. 64 (volleyball): Burazin/Photographer's Choice/GettyImages; p. 64 (goggles): Image Source/Image Source/GettyImages; p. 64 (football): Image Source/Image Source/GettyImages; p. 64 (hockey): C Squared Studios/Photodisc/GettyImages; p. 64 (baseball): PhotoObjects.net/PhotoObjects.net/GettyImages; p. 64 (basketball): Andrew Dernie/Stockbyte/GettyImages; p. 64 (skates): RedKoalaDesign/iStock/GettyImages; p. 64 (snowboard): Stockbyte/Stockbyte/GettyImages; p. 64 (bike): hamurishi/iStock/GettyImages; p. 64 (hiking boots): Don Bayley/E+/GettyImages; p. 64 (soccer): Lazi & Mellenthin/Westend61/GettyImages; p. 64 (BR): Blend Images - Jose Luis Pelaez Inc/Brand X Pictures/GettyImages; p. 64 (Victor): Blend Images - Jose Luis Pelaez Inc/Brand X Pictures/GettyImages; p. 64 (Tara): Tom Merton/Caiaimage/GettyImages; p. 65 (T): Michael DeYoung/Design Pics/First Light/GettyImages; p. 65 (B): Lewis Mulatero/Taxi/GettyImages; p. 66 (T): Jupiterimages/Stone/GettyImages; p. 66 (B): shaunl/iStock/Getty Images Plus/GettyImages; p. 67 (Ex 7.a.1): Alexander Rhind/Stone/GettyImages; p. 67 (Ex 7.a.2): leaf/iStock/Getty Images Plus/GettyImages; p. 67 (Ex 7.a.3): innovatedcaptures/iStock/Getty Images Plus/GettyImages; p. 67 (Ex 7.a.4): Spaces Images/Blend Images/GettyImages; p. 67 (Ex 7.a.5): alfalfa126/Moment/GettyImages; p. 67 (Ex 7.a.6): Gazimal/The Image Bank/GettyImages; p. 68 (Ex 9.1): Nicola Tree/Taxi/GettyImages; p. 68 (Ex 9.2): Westend61/Westend61/GettyImages; p. 68 (Ex 9.3): MarioGuti/iStock/GettyImages; p. 68 (Ex 9.4): Kyle Monk/Blend Images/GettyImages; p. 68 (Ex 9.5): Chad Springer/Image Source/GettyImages; p. 68 (Ex 9.6): olegkalina/iStock/GettyImages; p. 68 (Ex 9.7): Roberto Cerruti/Hemera/GettyImages; p. 68 (Ex 9.8): Tatomm/iStock/GettyImages; p. 69 (TL): Carlos Osorio/Toronto Star/GettyImages; p. 69 (Centre): SAM PANTHAKY/AFP/GettyImages; p. 69 (TR): Raul Sifuentes/Guiness World Records/Newscom; p. 71 (chef): Jetta Productions/Iconica/GettyImages; p. 71 (mechanic): Tanya Constantine/Blend Images/GettyImages; p. 71 (artist): Lisa Stirling/The Image Bank/GettyImages; p. 71 (musician): Hill Street Studios/Blend Images/GettyImages; p. 72 (header), p. viii (unit 11): Caiaimage/Tom Merton/Caiaimage/GettyImages; p. 72 (BR): Dorling Kindersley/Dorling Kindersley/GettyImages; p. 72 (Ava): LWA/Larry Williams/Blend Images/GettyImages; p. 72 (Martin): Marcos Ferro/GettyImages; p. 73 (Ex 3.a.1): Dave and Les Jacobs/Lloyd Dobbie/Blend Images/GettyImages; p. 73 (Ex 3.a.2): Mike Svoboda/DigitalVision/GettyImages; p. 73 (Ex 3.a.3): Kathrin Ziegler/Taxi/GettyImages; p. 73 (Ex 3.a.4): UpperCut Images/UpperCut Images/GettyImages; p. 73 (Ex 3.a.5): Jetta Productions/Iconica/GettyImages; p. 73 (Ex 3.a.6): Caiaimage/Paul Bradbury/OJO+/GettyImages; p. 73 (Ex 3.a.7): Nicolas McComber/E+/GettyImages; p. 73 (Ex 3.a.8): John Eder/The Image Bank/GettyImages; p. 74 (Morgan): Image Source/Image Source/GettyImage; p. 74 (Issac): T.T./Iconica/GettyImages; p. 74 (Lauren): PeopleImages/DigitalVision/GettyImages; p. 74 (Brian): Eugenio Marongiu/Cultura/GettyImages; p. 74 (Ex 7: photo1): tiridifilm/E+/GettyImages; p. 74 (Ex 7: photo2): Gail Shumway/Photographer's Choice/GettyImages; p. 74 (Ex 7: photo3): Zeb Andrews/Moment/GettyImages; p. 74 (Ex 7: photo4): PeopleImages.com/DigitalVision/GettyImages; p. 74 (Ex 7: photo5): Tetra Images/Tetra images/GettyImages; p. 74 (Ex 7: photo6): Rudi Von Briel/Photolibrary/GettyImages; p. 75 (Allie): Louise Morgan/Moment/Getty Images; p. 75 (Jim): Louise Morgan/Moment/Getty Images; p. 75 (TR): Vegar Abelsnes Photography/Photodisc/GettyImages; p. 76 (special cloth): William Tang/Design Pics/Perspectives/GettyImages; p. 76 (food): Ronnie Kaufman/Larry Hirshowitz/Blend Images/GettyImages; p. 76 (decorate): Photo by Glenn Waters in Japan/Moment/GettyImages; p. 76 (give gifts): Fastrum/iStock/GettyImages; p. 76 (play music): Derek E. Rothchild/Photolibrary/GettyImages; p. 76 (parade): Oliver Strewe/Lonely Planet Images/GettyImages; p. 76 (picnic): uniquely india/photosindia/GettyImages; p. 76 (fireworks): Ichiro Murakami/EyeEm/EyeEm/GettyImages; p. 76 (blossom festival): Bohistock/Moment/GettyImages; p. 76 (carnival): Yadid Levy/robertharding/robertharding/GettyImages; p. 77 (TL): Foodcollection RF/Foodcollection/GettyImages; p. 77 (CR): Emilia Krysztofiak Rua Photography/Moment/GettyImages; p. 77 (BL): Thomas Fricke/First Light/GettyImages; p. 77 (BR): Kelly Cheng Travel Photography/Moment Open/GettyImages; p. 78 (header), p. viii (unit 12): Mark Alcarez/Photolibrary/GettyImages; p. 78 (man): Eric Audras/ONOKY/GettyImages; p. 78 (holding volleyball): Stockbyte/GettyImages; p. 80 (Ex 4.a.1): Predrag Vuckovic/iStock/GettyImages; p. 80 (Ex 4.a.2): Ghislain & Marie David de Lossy/Cultura/GettyImages; p. 80 (Ex 4.a.3): Lawren/Moment/GettyImages; p. 80 (Ex 4.a.4): g-stockstudio/iStock/GettyImages; p. 80 (chamomile tea): Maximilian Stock Ltd./Photographer's Choice/GettyImages; p. 80 (cough syrup): Comstock/Stockbyte/GettyImages; p. 80 (chicken soup): Shawn Gearhart/E+/GettyImages; p. 80 (cold medicine): MakiEni's photo/Moment Open/GettyImages; p. 80 (eye drops): BananaStock/BananaStock/GettyImages; p. 80 (aspirin): Diane Macdonald/Photographer's Choice RF/GettyImages; p. 80 (antacid): STEVE HORRELL/SPL/Science Photo Library/GettyImages; p. 80 (nasal spray): hamikus/iStock/GettyImages; p. 80 (ice pack): Hero Images/Hero Images/GettyImages; p. 81: Chad Baker/Jason Reed/Ryan McVay/Photodisc/GettyImages; p. 82 (Ex 10.a.1): diego_cervo/iStock/GettyImages; p. 82 (Ex 10.a.2): BSIP/UIG/Universal Images Group/GettyImages; p. 82 (Ex 10.a.3): Garry Wade/The Image Bank/GettyImages; p. 82 (Ex 10.a.4): ViewStock/View Stock/GettyImages; p. 83: pixologicstudio/iStock/Getty Images Plus/GettyImages; p. 85 (TL): Paul Bradbury/OJO Images/GettyImages; p. 85 (TC): BartekSzewczyk/iStock/GettyImages; p. 85 (TR): Image Source/Photodisc/GettyImages; p. 85 (BL): baona/iStock/GettyImages; p. 85 (BC): Manuel Faba Ortega/iStock/GettyImages; p. 85 (BR): Jamie Grill/The Image Bank/GettyImages; p. 86 (header), p. viii (unit 13): Andy Ryan/Stone/GettyImages; p. 86 (Ex 1.a.a): Tetra Images/Tetra images/GettyImages; p. 86 (Ex 1.a.b): Musketeer/DigitalVision/GettyImages; p. 86 (Ex 1.a.c): PhotoAlto/James Hardy/Brand X Pictures/GettyImages; p. 86 (Ex 1.a.d): Bloomberg/Bloomberg/GettyImages; p. 86 (Ex 1.a.e): Deborah Cheramie/iStock/GettyImages; p. 86 (Ex 1.a.f): Jetta Productions/The Image Bank/GettyImages; p. 86 (Ex 1.a.g): Inti St Clair/Blend Images/GettyImages; p. 86 (Ex 1.a.h): David Nevala/Aurora/GettyImages; p. 89 (TL): David Henderson/Caiaimage/GettyImages; p. 89 (TC): Chris Mellor/Lonely Planet Images/GettyImages; p. 89 (TR): Medioimages/Photodisc/Photodisc/GettyImages; p. 89 (BL): Cultura RM Exclusive/Christoffer Askman/Cultura Exclusive/GettyImages; p. 89 (BC): STAN HONDA/AFP Creative/GettyImages; p. 89 (BR): Chris Mellor/Lonely Planet Images/GettyImages; p. 91 (TL): Fandrade/Moment/GettyImages; p. 91 (TC): Anton Petrus/Moment/GettyImages; p. 91 (TR): Karina Vera/Moment/GettyImages; p. 91 (CL): Rebeca Mello/Moment Open/GettyImages; p. 91 (BL): Bettmann/Bettmann/GettyImages; p. 91 (BR): Alfredo Herms/STR/LatinContent WO/GettyImages; p. 92 (header), p. viii (unit 14): Adam Burton/robertharding/GettyImages; p. 92 (Ex 1: photo 1): Caiaimage/Paul Bradbury/Riser/GettyImages; p. 92 (Ex 1: photo 2): Maskot/GettyImages; p. 92 (Ex 1: photo 3): Fabrice LEROUGE/ONOKY/GettyImages; p. 92 (Ex 1: photo 4): Holger Mette/iStock/Getty Images Plus/GettyImages; p. 92 (Ex 1: photo 5): Ariel Skelley/Blend Images/GettyImages; p. 92 (Ex 1: photo 6): David Jakle/Image Source/GettyImages; p. 92 (Ex 1: photo 7): Andersen Ross/Blend Images/GettyImages; p. 92 (Ex 1: photo 8): Hero Images/GettyImages; p. 92 (BR): Absodels/ABSODELS/GettyImages; p. 93: A. Chederros/ONOKY/GettyImages; p. 94 (TL): Djura Topalov/iStock/Getty Images Plus/GettyImages; p. 94 (TC): JGI/Jamie Grill/Blend Images/GettyImages; p. 94 (TR): KNSY/Picture Press/GettyImages; p. 94 (CL): svetikd/E+/GettyImages; p. 94 (C): Ghislain & Marie David de Lossy/Cultura/GettyImages; p. 94 (CR): Kevin Kozicki/Image Source/GettyImages; p. 95 (TR): Greg Elms/Lonely Planet Images/GettyImages; p. 95 (Kim): Sam Edwards/Caiaimage/GettyImages; p. 95 (Martin): Jetta Productions/Blend Images/GettyImages; p. 95 (BR): Thomas Barwick/Taxi/GettyImages; p. 96: Matthew Micah Wright/Lonely Planet Images/GettyImages; p. 97 (Nick): William King/The Image Bank/GettyImages; p. 97 (Jessie): Caiaimage/Sam Edwards/OJO+/GettyImages; p. 97 (Armando): Daniel Ernst/iStock/Getty Images Plus/GettyImages; p. 97 (Juliette): Robert Daly/Caiaimage; p. 99 (T): David Wall Photo/Lonely Planet Images/GettyImages; p. 99 (C): Emma Innocenti/Taxi/GettyImages; p. 99 (B): Robert Deutschman/DigitalVision/GettyImages; p. 100 (header), p. viii (unit 15): David Oliver/The Image Bank/GettyImages; p. 100 (Ex 1.1): Jeff Kravitz/FilmMagic, Inc/GettyImages; p. 100 (Ex 1.2): Gary Gershoff/WireImage/GettyImages; p. 100 (Ex 1.3): Bruce Glikas/FilmMagic/GettyImages; p. 100 (Ex 1.4): G Fiume/Getty Images Sport/GettyImages; p. 100 (Ex 1.5): Kevork Djansezian/Getty Images News/GettyImages; p. 102 (TR): John Eder/The Image Bank/GettyImages; p. 104: Ridofranz/iStock/GettyImages; p. 105 (map): Richard Sharrocks/iStock/Getty Images Plus/GettyImages; p. 105 (boy): Tim Kitchen/DigitalVision/GettyImages; p. 105 (B/G): Mark Miller Photos/Photolibrary/GettyImages; p. 106 (header), p. viii (unit 16): Lumina Images/Blend Images; p. 106 (CL): PhotoAlto/Frederic Cirou/PhotoAlto Agency RF Collections/GettyImages; p. 106 (CR): Caiaimage/Sam Edwards/Caiaimage/GettyImages; p. 106 (BL): REB Images/Blend Images/GettyImages; p. 106 (BR): Gary Burchell/Taxi/

GettyImages; p. 106 (BR): Cultura RM Exclusive/Gary John Norman/Cultura Exclusive/GettyImages; p. 107: Marc Romanelli/Blend Images/GettyImages; p. 108 (camping): Hero Images/Hero Images/GettyImages; p. 108 (amusement park): Joe McBride/Iconica/GettyImages; p. 108 (street fair): Patti McConville/Photographer's Choice/GettyImages; p. 108 (concert): PeopleImages.com/DigitalVision/GettyImages; p. 108 (barbecue): Hero Images/Hero Images/GettyImages; p. 108 (play): Caiaimage/Robert Daly/OJO+/GettyImages; p. 108 (Nathan): Ezra Bailey/Taxi/GettyImages; p. 108 (Julie): Mike Chick/Stone/GettyImages; p. 108 (BR): Image Source/Image Source/GettyImages; p. 109: NT Photography/Image Source/GettyImages; p. 110 (TR): B Busco/Photographer's Choice/GettyImages; p. 110 (BR): monkeybusinessimages/iStock/GettyImages; p. 111 (T): Cooper Neill/Getty Images Entertainment/GettyImages; p. 112 (Audrey Hepburn): Michael Ochs Archives/Moviepix/GettyImages; p. 112 (Nelson Mandela): Per-Anders Pettersson/Hulton Archive/GettyImages; p. 112 (Paul Walker): Jason Merritt/FilmMagic/GettyImages; p. 113: PeopleImages/DigitalVision/GettyImages; p. 123 (almonds): Ljupco/iStock/GettyImages; p. 123 (vegetables): Bill Arce/StockFood Creative/GettyImages; p. 123 (cake): bluestocking/E+/GettyImages; p. 123 (candy): Diana Taliun/iStock/GettyImages; p. 123 (chocolates): pilcas/iStock/GettyImages; p. 123 (cookies): bluestocking/E+/GettyImages; p. 123 (chips): sunstock/iStock/GettyImages; p. 123 (grapes): Donald Erickson/E+/GettyImages; p. 123 (hot dogs): IngaNielsen/iStock/GettyImages; p. 123 (Icecream): Donald Erickson/E+/GettyImages; p. 123 (peanuts): Suwanmanee99/iStock/GettyImages; p. 123 (pineapple): Marek Mnich/E+/GettyImages; p. 123 (pizza): david franklin/E+/GettyImages; p. 123 (popcorn): Korovin/iStock/GettyImages; p. 123 (potato chips): rimglow/iStock/GettyImages; p. 123 (watermelon): mkos83/iStock/GettyImages; p. 124 (CL): Brand New Images/Stone/GettyImages; p. 124 (C): Hero Images/Hero Images/GettyImages; p. 124 (CR): Westend61/Westend61/GettyImages; p. 124 (BL): Tara Moore/The Image Bank/GettyImages; p. 124 (BC): Ron Krisel/Stone/GettyImages; p. 124 (BR): Art Vandalay/Photodisc/GettyImages; p. 125 (remote): Gary Ombler/Dorling Kindersley/GettyImages; p. 125 (cheese): Thomas Firak Photography/Photolibrary/GettyImages; p. 125 (BR): Ian Logan/The Image Bank/GettyImages; p. 125 (clock): Korvit78/iStock/GettyImages; p. 125 (BC): arkady2013/iStock/Getty Images Plus/GettyImages; p. 125 (BL): Sally Anscombe/Moment/GettyImages; p. 126 (car): Pgiam/E+/GettyImages; p. 126 (woman sleeping): Tanya Constantine/Blend Images/GettyImages; p. 126 (man): PeopleImages/E+/GettyImages; p. 126 (girl clicking): Plume Creative/DigitalVision/GettyImages; p. 129 (BR): Inti St Clair/Blend Images/GettyImages; p. 129 (BL): David Young-Wolff/The Image Bank/GettyImages; p. 129 (TL): Wavebreakmedia/iStock/GettyImages; p. 129 (CL): Jonathan Kirn/The Image Bank/GettyImages; p. 130 (TL): JGI/Tom Grill/Blend Images/GettyImages; p. 130 (TC): Tetra Images - Erik Isakson/Brand X Pictures/GettyImages; p. 130 (TR): AlenPopov/iStock/GettyImages; p. 130 (CL): Thinkstock/Stockbyte/GettyImages; p. 130 (C): Debbie Fortes/EyeEm/EyeEm/GettyImages; p. 130 (CR): Monashee Frantz/OJO Images/GettyImages; p. 130 (BL): George Doyle/Stockbyte/GettyImages; p. 130 (BC): Erik Isakson/Tetra images/GettyImages; p. 130 (BR): DamianPalus/iStock/GettyImages.